Grit, Resilience, and Motivation in Early Childhood

Grit, Resilience, and Motivation in Early Childhood moves past current media buzz about grit, resilience, and motivation as proverbial silver bullets and provides early childhood educators with a much-needed focus on developmentally appropriate activities and expectations related to those terms. Illustrated with classroom case studies, caregiver and community resources, and teacher behaviors, this powerful guide presents practical applications for educators to more deeply understand the research that will strengthen and support young children.

Lisa B. Fiore, Ph.D., is a professor of Early Childhood Education and Director of the Child Homelessness Initiative at Lesley University in Cambridge, Massachusetts.

Other Eye On Education Books
Available From Routledge
(www.routledge.com/eyeoneducation)

Grit, Resilience, and Motivation in Early Childhood

Practical Takeaways for Teachers

Lisa B. Fiore

Routledge
Taylor & Francis Group

NEW YORK AND LONDON

First published 2019
by Routledge
711 Third Avenue, New York, NY 10017

and by Routledge
2 Park Square, Milton Park, Abingdon, Oxon, OX14 4RN

Routledge is an imprint of the Taylor & Francis Group, an informa business

© 2019 Taylor & Francis

Library of Congress Cataloging-in-Publication Data
A catalog record for this book has been requested

ISBN: 978-1-138-08576-3 (hbk)
ISBN: 978-1-138-08577-0 (pbk)
ISBN: 978-1-315-11122-3 (ebk)

Typeset in Palatino
by Apex CoVantage, LLC

This book is lovingly dedicated to Kona, whose persistence and joyful invitations to play remind me daily that the secret to happiness can be summed up in one word: cheese.

Contents

Figures

Preface

Early childhood educators often grapple with the pressure to honor and value children as individuals and to prepare them for what society expects them to become. The passion that draws people to the profession is sometimes tested, and teachers may question their own abilities to persist in spite of threats to the joy and wonder of childhood, such as increased mandates, assessments, and accountability measures.

Grit, Resilience, and Motivation in Early Childhood is intended to challenge some assumptions (implicit and explicit) about early childhood, specifically, and teaching and learning more broadly. The chapters focus on topics that respect who children are, not just what we want them to be, and how teachers can collaborate with families and community partners to bring children's potential into clearer, closer focus. As teachers read about how to strengthen children's internal fortitude and acknowledge differences from an asset, rather than deficit, perspective, they are fortifying their own resolve.

The ideas, examples, and stories contained between the covers of this book are the result of much research, conversation, and observation. Finding inspiration in the work of early childhood professionals is second only to the inspiration provided by children in educational settings. In this book, attention is given to child development and culturally sensitive, anti-bias practice and expectations, children's work, group interactions, and teacher behavior. These include:

- Constructing an understanding of grit, resilience, and motivation in early childhood
- Considering human qualities and conditions as risk and protective factors
- Illustrating concepts through case studies and interactive web-based examples, which anchor material presented in chapters

The case studies presented in the *A Closer Look* section of each chapter are all based on actual examples communicated to or witnessed by the author. These case studies have been fictionalized, with specific names and details changed to ensure confidentiality. Each case study presents a scenario from the perspective of a particular individual invested in early childhood education, such as a child, parent, teacher, and administrator. Furthermore, activities and resources provided at the end of each chapter provide readers with opportunities to extend concepts and connect ideas to practice, thereby promoting creativity and engagement with children inside and outside of the classroom context.

Empowering children to persist in the face of obstacles or adversity results in powerful shifts—to their own developmental trajectories and to the mindsets of educators and families who care about them. A society that deems children to be competent and curious citizens demonstrates this value system with investments in programs that result in short-term and long-term gains for *all* citizens. As readers consider their own goals in relation to strengths and risk factors that impact children and families, they will be better able to influence the field of early childhood education as advocates for and with children and families. This book is therefore an invitation for reflection, for connection, and for action.

Acknowledgments

This book is the result of several years of conversations focused on the well-being of young children, and I wish to thank editor Alex Masulis for his wisdom and guidance during all stages of manuscript development. As all of the stories contained within these chapters are drawn from the inspirational real-life work of very talented and compassionate people, I wish to acknowledge Mary Geisser and Becca Mason for the work they do with young children and pre-service teachers, and the courage they model, questioning their own biases and assumptions in the interest of teaching with integrity and heart. I also want to acknowledge the educators, administrators, and staff of the Belmont, MA, school district, who have made social-emotional learning a priority in the classrooms through ongoing, inclusive training and practice. Demonstrating a commitment to ensuring that all children feel known and valued in school requires time and resources, as well as a recalibration of priorities in an era of high-stakes testing and accountability. Putting children first matters.

As this book evolved, the support and enthusiasm of several brilliant, funny, and fiercely dedicated women had a tremendous impact on my own determination and my evolving understanding of concepts that are connected to multiple, interconnected domains. My thanks go out to Susan Carey, Catherine Koverola, Sonia Pérez-Villanueva, Janet Sauer, and Donna San Antonio for their tremendous friendship—I am grateful to know you, laugh with you, and travel with you. The journey is much spicier because of you. I would especially like to acknowledge students Eva Bloche, Allie Gurrieri, Hannah Slattery, Yirui Su, and Iliana Valentin, whose generous and inquisitive spirits will inspire children in classroom and clinical settings, though they are already inspirational in their approaches to doing and being.

Finally, I would like to thank Steve, Matthew, and Talia for their encouragement, love, and patience. There is no greater motivation than seeing your smiles at the beginning and end of every day.

1

What's Going On Here?

You've got this.

Three words make up a simple statement—shorter than most fortune cookie fortunes—that conveys confidence, faith, and trust in one compact sentence. Why is it so challenging for some children to embody or internalize this same sentiment? And what is the role of teachers in supporting children's learning and development in a societal climate that emphasizes competition, assessment, and accountability? It is hard to be a teacher. And it is definitely harder today than when John Dewey (1916) was writing about education and democratic ideals. Following the format of Margaret Wise Brown's (1977) *The Important Book*, we could argue that the important thing about hard things is that they are hard. It is hard for teachers to balance the demands of work inside and out of the classroom, which includes increased attention on school violence and other sources of stress, and we know that children find it hard to be a student, too. They know it and they feel it.

Hard Things

Data indicates a significant increase in school violence for schools around the world (Benbenishty & Astor, 2014), and children in grades as early as preschool are—directly or indirectly—impacted by stress related to bullying, gangs, drug use/abuse, and standardized testing.

A recent article titled "Baby PISA Is Just Around the Corner, so Why Is No One Talking About It?" (Wasmuth, 2017) presents information about plans already underway, coordinated by the international Organization for Economic Cooperation and Development (OECD). These plans include a research study—the International Early Learning and Child Wellbeing Study—that will "gather information on children's cognitive and social-emotional skills" (p. 1) as well as "measure domains of emerging literacy and numeracy, executive function, and empathy and trust" (p. 1) through direct assessment. And furthermore, "[c]hildren will be expected to do their work on a tablet" (p. 1).

Early childhood educators, and educators at all levels of schooling who believe in educating the "whole child," recognize that academic achievement is influenced by some skills that are simply not measurable, or rather don't fit neatly into a determinate design. Rightly so. Yet categories have emerged in which discernable skills have been assigned as either academic skills or "soft" skills. Notice that it's not "hard" versus "soft" skills, though that is absolutely the connotation, and the implied message is that academic skills contain more rigor, density, and value. Other familiar terms for these categories are "cognitive" versus "noncognitive" skills, which imply that the academic skills reside in the head and the soft skills reside someplace else. Experts in research and policy argue that "noncognitive" skills, also referred to as "social-emotional" skills, "are linked to academic achievement, productivity, and collegiality . . . positive health indicators, and civic participation" (García & Weiss, 2017, p. 1) and are critical to children's overall health and well-being.

It is therefore no surprise that qualities such as *grit*, *resilience*, and *motivation* have gained renewed, increased attention—crossing discipline boundaries and influencing practices in fields such as psychology, sociology, and education. For those who are curious, it is interesting to notice the blurred lines that exist, leading to some confusion about the relationship between science and education, for example. What appears to be proven in scientific research may not translate effectively into classroom practice, and what "success" looks like in one context may look very different in another context, and may require resources and supports specific to a community, classroom, and individual. By its very nature, any blueprint or roadmap leads to an end that is already known, and human development simply does not work according to such guides, though history, experience, and the wisdom of experts in a variety of forms greatly inform the journey.

Misperceptions about early childhood education and what it takes to succeed complicate the already challenging educational terrain. For example, in his best-selling book, *How Children Succeed*, author Paul Tough states, "Most early childhood classrooms in the United States today are designed to develop in children a set of specific pre-academic skills, mostly related to deciphering text and manipulating numbers" (Tough, 2012, p. xii). He goes on to cite a curriculum, Tools of the Mind, with interventions designed to help children learn skills that include "controlling their impulses, staying focused on the task at hand, avoiding distractions and mental traps, managing their emotions, [and] organizing their thoughts" (p. xii). If I were using this paragraph as a reading in a college class of pre-service teachers, I would ask them to highlight or underline words/phrases that strike them as interesting, puzzling, and/or worth exploring together, identifying and challenging our own assumptions, as well as those of the author. After an initial, critical challenge to the statement about "most" early childhood classrooms in the U.S., questions that might arise include:

How do we define pre-academic? *Are we not born ready to learn?*
What happens when behaviors fall outside of specific,
     predetermined skills? *How do we encourage creativity and
     flexibility?*
What skills matter? *Who decides?*

"Truly believing in the potential of all students requires changes in daily practices that are deeply embedded in school culture" (Krovetz, 2008, p. x). Early childhood educators do not enter the profession because of a love of hard things. They enter the profession because of a love of children, children's thinking, learning, playing, and ways of seeing and understanding the world. They would argue that most early childhood classrooms invite children to explore the way the world is *now* and to question *why* that is so. This stance toward teaching and learning is consistent with Ian Gilbert's (2014) writing about independent thinking, where teachers "open [students'] minds to question, to reflect, to look beneath the surface, to have beliefs that they will fight for and fight for the beliefs of others, even if they don't agree with them" (p. 155).

Early childhood educators possess dispositions that tend toward an acceptance of difference, an inquisitive spirit, and a comfort with mess because of a conviction that process is as important—if not more so—as products in revealing children's innate competence. Educator and children's advocate Erika Christakis (2016) argues:

Today's children will one day grow up; more children will come and go. And as each successive wave leaves childhood behind, they become the adults who misread and misunderstand the latest batch of arrivals, who are patiently waiting for us to see them as they truly are.

(p. 297)

Focusing Our Own Lenses on Grit, Resilience, and Motivation

Throughout this book, vignettes are presented to provide opportunities to focus early childhood educators' lenses on ordinary, lived experiences, and to notice the grit, resilience, and motivation inherent in each story. As you begin to focus your own "noticing" skills in new ways, you will likely notice that while the terms *grit, resilience*, and *motivation* are often used synonymously, there are subtle, distinct differences between the terms. These differences can guide decisions about teaching practices and advocacy in your own context. And because every classroom possesses a unique combination of individuals and resources, it is helpful to get a sense of the broader context against which definitions may be examined and challenged.

Recent demographics in the United States suggest that a hypothetical classroom population would include students possessing the following qualities:

7 out of 30 live in poverty
11 out of 30 are non-white
6 out of 30 do not speak English as a first language
6 out of 30 are not reared by their biological parents
1 out of 30 are experiencing homelessness
6 out of 30 are victims of abuse

(Sultan, 2015)

While teacher education programs strive to provide students with knowledge and skills to best equip them for classroom teaching, no one licensure or certification program can encapsulate all of the challenges and design comprehensive strategies that will address the needs of all learners equally. Once this is acknowledged as a fact, educators who embrace a practice of lifelong learning for learning's sake are themselves modeling grit, resilience, and motivation for children, families, administrators, and community members. In the chapters that follow, each term will be presented in detail. The terms will be discussed briefly here, to establish a framework in which the concepts are understood not as traits, but instead as reflections of systems at work in every child's life—internal and external. Guiding questions that help anchor this framework include:

◆ How can early childhood educators recognize these qualities as they are manifested in the classroom?
◆ How can we teach children skills to develop and enhance these qualities?
◆ How can early childhood educators collaborate with others to improve systems that already exist?

Grit

Ask people to make an association with the word "grit," and words that come to mind often include "tough," "persistence," "fortitude," and "never give up," to name a few common terms. People also don't tend to associate the term with young children, as they imagine strong, often male characters, who may or may not be dirty! It's no surprise that many people also reference the famous Western film featuring John Wayne—*True Grit* (Nathan, Wallis, & Hazen, 1969). It's a pleasure to consider the main character of the film—a young girl named Mattie Ross—who sets out to avenge her father's death and finds assistance on her mission. She states with absolute conviction, "You must pay for everything in this world, one way and another. There is nothing free except the grace of G-d."

In the popular media circles, psychologist Angela Duckworth's (2016) writing and lectures (see www.ted.com/talks/angela_lee_duckworth_grit_the_power_of_passion_and_perseverance) have brought much attention to this term. The most appealing premise of the work is that grit can be taught, and if more people learn how to be gritty, they will be more successful. This assumes they will be happier as well, and perhaps enjoy fulfilling careers. Some concepts that are linked with the concept of grit—much like how atoms make up molecules—are persistence and delay of gratification. These will be discussed in Chapter 2, but the relevant characteristic is the ability to persist when faced with frustration, or even when obstacles seem particularly overwhelming. Some specific strategies that have been identified in research (e.g., Dacey, Mack, & Fiore, 2016) about persistence include:

Tolerating ambiguity or the unknown
Learning to take moderate risks
Acquiring a sense of personal courage
Valuing delay of gratification
Avoiding rigid thinking
Avoiding "drift"

The notion that children can be taught to develop/possess grit holds tremendous promise for people concerned about the levels of stress and anxiety that continue to increase among adolescents, and the competitive global landscape that we are reminded about constantly. So a term that was anchored in psychological research has become adopted by other fields, such as sociology and education. This has led to some concern and criticism expressed by experts in those fields. For example, in educational settings, administrators and teachers have begun using "grit" as common parlance that means "sticking it out." Children have begun recognizing moments when they persist as "gritty." In this manner, critics argue that the main impetus for teaching children to be gritty is to promote academic achievement. Prominent authors and education advocates encourage educators and caregivers to reflect on other possible goals for children, such as helping them to lead healthy lives infused with integrity and creativity (Kohn, 2014).

For example, author and advocate Alfie Kohn (2014) writes:

> when students throw up their hands after failing at something they were asked to do, it may be less because they lack grit than because they weren't really "asked" to do it—they were told to do it. They had nothing to say about the content or context of the curriculum. And people of all ages are more likely to persevere when they have a chance to make decisions about the things that affect them.
>
> (par. 23)

The concern is echoed by Linda Nathan, who emphasizes the inequities that children experience related to economic resources in schools and poverty in general. She argues that when children do not succeed (and what this means is different to different people in different contexts), blame is cast upon "the student rather than a system that is inherently unfair and inequitable" (Nathan, 2017, p. 6). Nathan articulates five assumptions that frame students' successes and failures:

1. Money doesn't have to be an obstacle
2. Race doesn't matter
3. Just work harder
4. There is a college for everyone/everyone can go to college
5. If you believe in yourself, your dreams will come true

It is with a critical—and sometimes skeptical—eye toward improving and strengthening lives for all children and families that educators must be committed to changing the systems that impact children's learning and development, rather than trying to imbue children with some qualities or characteristics that will allow them to persist and ultimately overcome adversity.

Resilience

Positive adaptation in spite of adversity is precisely how the term resilience has been defined in psychological research for well over 40 years. In these decades, the focus was primarily on the individual.

> Resilience research has gone through several stages. From an initial focus on the invulnerable or invincible child, psychologists began to recognize that much of what seems to promote resilience originates outside of the individual. This led to a search for resilience factors at the individual, family, community—and, most recently, cultural—levels.
>
> (Fleming & Ledogar, 2008, p. 7)

In their seminal research on the island of Kauai, Emmy Werner and Ruth Smith noted lessons learned about resilience across an individual's lifetime:

> The lessons we learned from an examination of the process that linked each of these protective buffers together over time were twofold: *first*, the extraordinary importance of the (early) childhood years in laying the foundation for resilience, and *second*, the possibilities for recovery at later stages in development that were available to most individuals who seized the opportunities offered to them by naturally occurring support systems in the community.
>
> (Werner & Smith, 2001, p. 172)

How might early childhood educators create support systems for children and families? The encouraging news is that children who are exposed to risk factors, such as trauma, homelessness, or family dysfunction, are not doomed to failure and major problems later in life. The researchers found that at each developmental stage, opportunities exist for protective factors to thwart the negative impact of negative factors (Werner & Smith, 2001).

Psychologist Ann Masten (2015) has concluded that such protective factors include:

Capable caregiving and parenting and other close relationships
Problem-solving skills, self-regulation skills, and self-efficacy
Faith, hope, and belief that life has meaning
Effective schools (especially early childhood education),
    communities, and cultural practices

Masten also cites motivation to succeed as an important factor, and this will be discussed below, as well as in Chapter 4.

So is resilience *what* a child possesses or does, or is it more than that? Is it an internal state or an external system? A common question that researchers ask is whether experience with adversity helps or impedes a child's capacity to adapt. In a recent casual conversation with a parent, the mother shared a story of her son's latest swim meet. She noted that swimmers on the opposing team seemed to have worked quite hard to excel—these swimmers were from a school in a less economically advantaged town. She believed that the students on this particular swim team were able to achieve in spite of the economic adversity assumed to exist in that community. She laughed wryly, saying, "I wish my kid had a hardship!" She expressed mild concern that her son didn't have as much to overcome in the present/short term that would ultimately make him stronger in the long term. She perceived the swimmers on the opposing team to have fought hard and risen above the challenges to get to this point, and therefore seemed really strong.

The story reflects values inherent in an individual and supported by a community and greater society. What are we looking for when we notice and celebrate resilience? Children identified as "high-risk" as early as age 2—and who grew into adults without any major problems—were described by independent observers (psychologists and pediatricians) with adjectives denoting a positive social orientation, compared with high-risk children who later experienced problems at age 40 (Werner & Smith, 2001). Positive descriptors included adjectives such as agreeable, cheerful, friendly, responsive, self-confident, and sociable, whereas children who later developed problems were described in negative terms such as anxious, bashful, fearful, suspicious, or withdrawn.

If the concept of resilience is shifted from an individual to a community, such as a school community, where all staff take collective responsibility for student learning, then children become "problem-solvers and not problems to be solved" (Krovetz, 2008, p. 87). Parents, students, administrators, the central office, and the state and federal departments of education, as well as all taxpayers, compose the educational community and are therefore motivated to help all children thrive.

Motivation

It is clear that the interplay between psychological, social, educational, economic, and other factors makes it difficult, if not impossible, to identify one pathway to happiness, success, or prosperity. It is equally challenging to define those terms in any tangible sense; however, human beings are inclined toward categorizing as we strive to make sense of the world.

In the education domain, success tends to be measured by standardized test scores and grades—variables that may be relatively quickly ascertained based on measures of predetermined outcomes.

> Good grades, in other words, are often just a sign of approval by the person with the power in a classroom . . . students who pursue higher grades tend to be less interested in what they're learning, more likely to think in a superficial fashion . . . and inclined to prefer the easiest possible task whenever they have a choice.
>
> (Kohn, 2014, par. 20)

What is less visible is the motivation that drives a child toward a specific goal. The concept of "locus of control" (Rotter, 1954) has been used to explain the extent to which a person believes they can control events around them. A person displays an internal locus of control if she believes she has some control over her own life. A person displays an external locus of control if she believes that her life is controlled by outside factors, such as luck or fate. Those who have a strong *internal* locus of control perceive that what happens in their lives results primarily from their own actions. People with a strong *external* locus of control tend to credit external forces or others for their successes or failures. A simple example is a child attempting to score a goal in her soccer game. A child with a strong internal locus of control will take credit for or blame herself for making or missing the goal (e.g., much practice vs. not enough practice), whereas a child with a strong external locus of control will blame other factors (e.g., stronger opponents, holes in the grass, shoes too small).

Similarly, a child's motivation to reach a goal—to succeed in a narrow or broader sense—may also be described as intrinsic or extrinsic. *Intrinsic* motivation refers to energy or desire coming from within the individual (e.g., "I really want to improve my piano skills because playing the piano makes me happy!"), and *extrinsic* motivation refers to forces outside the individual (e.g., demands, expectations, guilt, or rewards imposed by others) that may result in the same outcome. So while an outcome, such as a strong grade on a test or performance in a gymnastics competition, may look the same, how the child approached the goal and implemented steps necessary to achieve the goal may be very different and may cause a child greater and lesser degrees of discomfort.

There is something vitally important, then, about really and truly seeing children as individuals, listening to them, and honoring them for who they are. The children's book *"Slowly, Slowly, Slowly," Said the Sloth* by Eric Carle captures the essence of self-awareness and honoring who we each are as the title character responds to other animals:

> "It is true that I am slow, quiet
> and boring. I am lackadaisical,
> I dawdle and I dillydally.
> I am also unflappable, languid,
> stoic, impassive, sluggish,
> lethargic, placid, calm, mellow,
> laid-back and, well, slothful!
> I am relaxed and tranquil,
> and I like to live in peace.
> But I am not lazy."
> Then the sloth yawned and said,
> "That's just how I am.
> I like to do things
>   slowly,
>   slowly,
>   slowly."
>   (Carle, 2002)

As we consider grit, resilience, and motivation in early childhood, it is important to consider the contextual factors that color our own perceptions and influence our decisions.

Context, Competition, and Other Cs

What messages do we send to children about what we see? About what we value? About their potential? A quick online search of any five random schools' or school districts' mission statements (give it a try!) will undoubtedly include several of the following words that begin with the letter "c": communication, collaboration, critical thinking, college, career, core, common, community, and compete. Slightly less frequent are the words culture, create, and caring. These words are not worrisome by their very nature, and can, in fact, contribute to some fine haiku poetry. Complications arise when these words are imbued with values that are measured and—further—serve as a reflection of a school's success.

Figure 1.1 presents examples of signs displayed in the foyers of two schools—the public entrance halls used by children, families, and community members who enter these respective schools. The example on the left, "The Rights of Children," is the language used in the foyer of the Diana School in Reggio Emilia, Italy. The preschool is one of the municipal schools for children ages 3 to 5 years old. The example on the right is adapted from signage that is viewed by anyone entering a particular public elementary school in New England. Considering these two examples side by side, what messages do you glean from the sentiments expressed? What messages are conveyed about children's potential? How might these messages be interpreted by adults? Internalized by children? How might these messages affect children's motivation?

If educators want to improve the odds for young children in general, and to address access and equity in education directly, we need to approach *childhood* anew, and to begin by exploring how schools affect children, how qualities such as *grit, resilience,* and *motivation* are developed and sustained, and how society will invest in children's potential

The Rights of Children

Children have the right to have friends, otherwise they do not grow up too well.

Children have the right to live in peace.

To live in peace means to be well, to live together, to live with things that interest us, to have friends, to think about flying, to dream.

If a child does not know, she has the right to make mistakes. It works because after she sees the problem and the mistakes she made, then she knows.

We've got to have rights, or else we'll be sad.

(Diana School, 1990)

Neighborhood School
Teacher, Parent/Guardian, Student Handbook
School Year 2017-2018

Smart is not something you are; smart is something you GET
Effort = Success!!

Neighborhood School
Principal   Asst. Principal
Supervisor of Special Services

Figure 1.1 A Tale of Two Entryways

as the promise of a meaningful democracy. Research by a Nobel Prize–winning economist, Professor [James] Heckman at the University of Chicago, suggests that every dollar invested in very early services for children has a return in social savings or revenue. He estimates this return at approximately 7 or 8 dollars for every dollar investment (Lopez, 2017). What does such an investment look like? It could come in the form of support for social programs that support children *and* families. This two-tier investment accounts for high rankings in terms of childhood conditions and outcomes:

> Whether that's preschool services or after school and out of school activities as well as children's health issues, those are typically going to be the ones that have better outcomes, where kids are actually able to have a childhood that is a time where they can learn, grow, play, feel protected, feel safe and have the opportunity to really reach their full potential.
>
> (Lopez, 2017, p. 3)

Authors and researchers have long asked why some children succeed in the short and long term, and why some children fail. Why do some children thrive while others stumble? As early childhood educators, what can any of us do to guide individual children—or a whole classroom of children—toward identifying their passions and finding success in the broadest sense?

So how do we know what a child's full potential is? How are we defining success? How are we judging that potential and limiting some children while privileging others? Kohn explains the term "fundamental attribution error" as a tendency—often displayed by social psychologists and other influential researchers—to focus narrowly on concepts such as character, personality, and individual responsibility. He cautions that in doing so we often overlook the profound influence of the social environment and the very real effects that it has on children and education (Kohn, 2014). This sentiment is echoed by others:

> Children's experience of childhood is largely determined by the care and protection they receive, or fail to receive, from adults. Children have the right to survival, food and nutrition, health, and shelter. They also have the right to be encouraged and educated, both formally and informally. And they have the right to live free from fear, safe from violence and protected from abuse and exploitation.
>
> (Geoghan, 2017, p. 1)

Early childhood educators are not also trained to be therapists, and the role of "teacher" positions them as others—distinctly separate from parents or peers. Highly effective teachers scaffold children's learning and inquiry through an evolving understanding of the needs of the learners in their care. "They do their best to create the ideal mental and physical environment for their students' learning" (Rodriguez & Fitzpatrick, 2014, p. 69).

The desire to help all children achieve to the best of their abilities, and to increase these abilities along the way, means that teachers must first notice what obstacles stand in the way of children reaching specific goals, and what strengths—the children's and the teacher's—may be utilized to help children overcome obstacles along their educational pathway. Early childhood educators recognize that this pathway includes social and emotional learning, and that academic success cannot be separated from these other elements.

Social-Emotional Learning and Development

The work of psychologist Howard Gardner (1983), whose research on intelligence led to his theory of multiple intelligences, is often cited as contributing to the beginning of what is now more than a movement, but a distinct field of study and practice—social-emotional learning (SEL). Gardner's theory gained much appreciation from educators, who felt the theory resonated with what they knew and felt to be true. The theory challenged the long-held understanding—and acceptance as truth—that intelligence is one-dimensional, measurable through the use of standardized assessments, and something a person simply possesses to greater and lesser degrees, without consideration of myriad other factors. Gardner identified eight specific types of intelligences, and his later work suggested additional possible domains. Daniel Goleman's (2005) work on "emotional" intelligence further expanded the boundaries of what might be considered "intelligent" or "gifted." For example, you can likely think of someone who embodies a spirit that creates peace around them. Someone, for example, whose presence instantly makes others feel calmer, and whose spirit is kind and generous, inspiring others to be more thoughtful in kind. We might not immediately label this individual as a "genius," but this level of skill, insight, and/or empathy may indeed be considered such if we notice the lens through which we are perceiving an individual's abilities. "Decades of research in human development, cognitive and behavioral neuroscience, and educational practice and policy have illuminated that major domains of human development—social, emotional, cognitive, linguistic, academic—are deeply intertwined in the brain and in behavior. Moreover, all are central to learning and success" (Aspen Institute, 2017, p. 10).

The Collaborative for Academic, Social, and Emotional Learning (CASEL) (https://casel.org) has become a leading organization

Figure 1.2 Rainbow Boys

and resource for educators, families, and community providers who acknowledge the importance of social and emotional learning in human development. Anchored in research and informed by classroom application, CASEL identifies five competencies that contribute to increased positive impact on children's lives:

◆ Self-awareness—young children learn to recognize their own emotions and the emotions of others. They also learn how to manage or regulate these emotions.

◆ Self-management—this competency is often referenced when young children experience challenging or difficult circumstances (e.g., trauma, poverty), but applies to a general attitude or disposition as well (e.g., hopeful, courageous). Being able to adapt when times get tough is considered a key coping skill.

◆ Social awareness—young children express connections with and concern for others as early as infancy, and as they grow and develop language, this competency extends to others outside of their immediate social network. Children become better able to exercise care and concern as their experiences expose them to a wider variety of situations.

◆ Responsible decision-making—children typically learn from their mistakes as well as successes. As they gain more experience with situations that impact friendships, health and safety, and academic work, they build up their repertoire and have strategies to call upon when confronted with sometimes challenging decisions.

◆ Relationship skills—we are all born as innately social beings, so we begin to form relationships in our earliest moments. Over a lifetime, some relationships provide children with strength and validation, while some relationships are less positive, and children must learn lifelong skills such as talking *and* listening, asking for *and* giving help, and projecting confidence *and* allowing themselves to be vulnerable.

Teaching children is anchored in the relationships we form with children and families. Teaching children is enhanced when we take a look at ourselves. Early childhood educators need to carefully examine their own underlying beliefs about what compels them to get out of bed and go to work every morning, as well as their beliefs about children as learners. Together with colleagues who feel inspired to undertake similar careful examination, teachers can examine their own practices—through samples of students' work and other data—to learn more about how these beliefs translate into classroom culture and practice. The activities that follow are designed to promote reflection and increased awareness through close examination and looking at the ordinary in new ways.

Turning Ideas Into Action

Noticing What We Notice

Goal: To recalibrate and attune our senses through examination of ordinary objects

Materials needed: Three or four items that you carry with you or work with every day, in a work bag, backpack, or desk drawer

Action: Choose three or four items that you are quite familiar with, and place them before you on a table or someplace where you can examine them easily. As you look at the objects one by one, invite yourself to notice these items by features rather than by name or label. For example, what is something that you notice right away about the item? What color is it? Of what material(s) is it made? Notice the weight, smell, and feel of the items, one at a time. Hold the items up to the light to more closely examine the surface of each item. Does holding the item to the light create shadows, rainbows (prism/refraction), or other phenomena? If you shake or move the object, does it make a different sound than when it is still?

When you have examined each of the objects individually, see what you notice when you look at the objects in combination with each other. How do the objects complement each other? Are you naturally drawn to pairing or combining some objects and not others? How do you explain this? If you were to rename the objects, alone or in groupings, what name(s) would you create to identify the object(s)?

Extension: Do this same activity with a partner or small group of colleagues. As you each go through the exercise, share with each other observations that surprise you, challenge your long-held assumptions, and raise new questions. Reflect individually, taking a few minutes to write what you noticed, and then share these reflections together to gain multiple perspectives about the experience.

As you examine and explore these objects, notice how you may develop new appreciation for these items. Looking at items in a new way is analogous to noticing people in new lights. With this new awareness, your observation lenses will be sharper and less constricted by predictable definitions and expectations.

A New View

Goal: To look more closely at the details of a context with which you are very familiar, bringing these details into focus without bias or judgment

Materials needed: 3″ x 5″ (or 4″ x 6″) index cards, prepared with a 2″ x 2″ square cutout of the center of the cards; 8½″ x 11″ plain paper; pencils or pens

Action: The cutout portion of the index cards serves a function similar to that of a camera lens or telescope, providing a limited view of something upon which you are looking. Take the card with you on a classroom exploration, and look at the new "view" afforded by the square cutout. Choose one area in your classroom to focus on for approximately 10–15 minutes. Try to keep information that you know about the scene out of your mind as you notice *only* what is visible within the boundaries of the square cutout.

As you observe the new view, holding the card in one hand, use your other hand to loosely sketch a representation of the view onto a sheet of paper. The goal of this step is not to create a perfect representation of what you see, but to notice what you see within the boundaries of this viewfinder. The scale of what is represented within the view may not accurately reflect what exists in three-dimensional reality, and this is exactly as it should be.

As you observe and represent familiar details in new ways, you are gaining practice and skills that will translate into looking at children and their behaviors in new ways. It is through our closer examination of the ordinary that we learn to convey the extraordinary meanings to others, who may be less familiar with a philosophical stance that celebrates children's innate strengths, curiosities, and competence.

An Alien Lands on a Playground . . .

Goal: To observe children like a complete newcomer—imagine an alien or an anthropologist!

Materials needed: Notebook and/or sketchpad; pencils/pens

Action: Choose a location that could be described as a child's natural habitat—a park, a playground, a children's room in a public library or bookstore, a children's museum, or another area where children can play and explore freely. Find a spot where you can sit comfortably for a period of 10–15 minutes or longer. Using your notebook or sketchpad, record what you observe, focusing on how children connect with their surroundings, including people and objects.

As you observe, you may ask yourself questions such as:

◆ What elements in/of the space capture the child's/children's attention and interest?
◆ Do you notice a difference depending on the age of the children? Sex/gender preferences?
◆ What elements seem to provide children with joy? How is this joy conveyed to others, and how do others respond?
◆ What elements seem to challenge the children or stretch their thinking? How is frustration conveyed to others, and how do others respond?
◆ How is children's competence supported in this environment? How is it hindered or undermined?
◆ How does this space communicate to children their role(s) in the community?

At the end of your observation, take a minute or two to reflect upon your own feelings. Were there moments when you felt elated, frustrated, curious, or surprised? How does this observation inspire you to incorporate new elements or elevate/highlight existing elements in your own classroom space?

Extension: Share this experience with a friend or colleague. Share your reflections with each other and consider how your roles and responsibilities as educators are impacted by the experience, and how you might engage families in new understandings about children's competence and curiosity.

A Closer Look: Interplay Between Grit, Resilience, and Motivation

"Teachers always liked me," said Effie, smiling. "They called me *affable.*" She rolled her eyes and put the back of her hand to her forehead in a dramatic swoon-like posture. "I didn't even know what that *meant*! I just knew that I liked that they *knew* me."

Effie, now a sophomore in a teacher education program, wrote and spoke about her own memories of school as part of a class assignment. One of five children born to Puerto Rican parents who moved to Massachusetts when her older brothers were five and eight years old, Effie recalled life being complicated because of the family's financial situation, as well as the complexities that she experienced but didn't fully understand until she was in her early 20s.

"My older brothers were almost twenty years old by the time I was born, so it's almost like my parents had two families—my two brothers and then the rest of us." Effie described her relationship with her sister as strong, even though they "fight like crazy all the time." "What do you expect when you live in a house with eight people and *one* bathroom? *One* bathroom!" She said that she was always closest with her brother, who is six years older than her.

"I remember this one time I wanted to play with my brother, so I went into his room, like I always used to do, and I was like, 'Yo, dude? What's happening?' and he turned to me, and his eyes were really red and mad. He told me to get out. I was only eight, and I was hella stubborn, so I was like, 'No, really, dude! Play with me!' and he got up and pushed me—really hard. I fell back onto the wall and kind of stood there. I think I was just so confused. He stared at me, with this wicked cold expression on his face—I'll never forget it—and came toward me. He literally pushed me and pushed me until he pushed me out of his room and into the hallway. He shut the door and I was just left there, totally confused! I had no idea why he was so mad at me or what I did to tick him off."

Effie explained that only a couple of years ago, her mother told her that Effie's father had gone to prison for two years when she was 8 years old.

"He got caught up in some kind of shady scheme with this neighborhood dude, and of course it didn't work out. And then the next thing you know, my mom's a single parent for two years and she didn't even tell my sister and me because she didn't want to upset us. A few of my cousins knew, and I have *no idea* how they kept that secret, but they did."

"My mom told us that my dad was in Puerto Rico building a house and that he would be gone for two years. But actually he was in *jail*! It explains so much!" Effie exclaimed, moving her hands animatedly while she talked. "It explains why my brother was so mad that day and why he didn't—couldn't—talk to me. My mom told him not to say anything to my sister and me 'cause we were too young. So now I'm 8 years old and I know something's up. I can't understand why we only talk to Dad at certain times during the week, or why he sent Christmas presents to us in this weird box and the presents [sent as part of a prison social work program] weren't really things we would've asked for, or why my big brothers would come over and talk with my mom in hushed tones. I always thought that they were disappointed in me or something."

"The person I trusted most was my second-grade teacher," Effie said, smiling and nodding. "She led an after-school drama club and I always went to that. It was the only place where I knew I could put it all out there. It was a place where we shared something with them [the adults], and they never would have known what was going on in any of our lives otherwise."

Effie mused, "The teachers must go through lists of every single student in the school, grade level by grade level. Teachers that I never had would say 'hi' to me, and it was like, so cool!" She noted that even in high school, as an underclassman, when older students noticed her in a positive way, it really helped her feel more confident.

Effie has remained close with her second-grade teacher to this day, and she remembers asking her once, "Did you like when I talked in class because it made you laugh or because it made you *think*?" The teacher had thought about it, and after a few moments she replied, "Both!" Effie smiled and shrugged as she remembered the exchange.

"I didn't get it, but I knew I liked it!" she gushed. "I worked really hard in school, for the most part. The teachers who were nice to me got more of my attention than other teachers did, and I tried my best to do my work right for them. I think I wanted them to think I was a smart, strong student, and by performing well it would reflect well on them, too."

Effie realized that she had been twisting the strings on her hoodie around her finger and the strings were a bit tangled up. She extricated her finger and laughed, rolling her eyes again.

"See this sweatshirt?" she asked, pointing to the writing on her black hoodie, which featured the words "Good enough" and a red rose on the front. "That's what it's all about! You can only be your best self and believe in yourself. And if you don't believe in yourself, then it's really great when family or a teacher believes in you, because sometimes the little voices in your head can be really hard to shut down."

Resources

The Wonder of Learning

www.thewonderoflearning.com/?lang=en_GB

This website presents stunning visual examples of documentation from early childhood infant-toddler centers and preschools in Reggio Emilia, Italy, and around the world. The individual areas on the site promote children as capable, curious, and active learners. The traveling exhibition has received international attention and provided inspiration for educators, children, and families.

Network for Public Education

https://networkforpubliceducation.org/

This organization was founded in 2013 by Diane Ravitch and Anthony Cody, and it strives to promote, strengthen, and improve public schools today. The website features information and research addressing topics of interest and concern for anyone with interest in and connections to public education.

Making Learning Visible

http://mlvpz.org

This project is, at its core, a collaborative effort focused on "culture, values, and democracy." This website leads visitors to examples of documentation of students' and educators' learning, research about children and schools, and key questions and ideas to provoke further thinking and effect change in classroom and school communities.

References

Benbenishty, R., & Astor, R.A. (2014). *School violence in an international context: A call for global collaboration in research and prevention.* Retrieved from Ijvs.org/files/Revue-07/04.-Benbenishty-Ijvs-7.pdf

Brown, M.W. (1977). *The important book*. New York, NY: HarperCollins Publishers.

Carle, E. (2002). *"Slowly, slowly, slowly", said the sloth*. New York, NY: Puffin Books.

Christakis, E. (2016). *The importance of being little: What preschoolers really need from grownups*. New York, NY: Viking.

Dewey, J. (1916). *Democracy and education*. New York, NY: Macmillan.

Fleming, J., & Ledogar, R.J. (2008). Resilience, an evolving concept: A review of literature relevant to aboriginal research. *Pimatisiwin: Journal of Aboriginal and Indigenous Community Health, 6*(2), 7–23.

García, E., & Weiss, E. (2017). Making whole-child education the norm: How research and policy initiatives can make social and emotional skills a focal point of children's education. *Economic Policy Institute.* Retrieved from www.epi.org/publication/making-whole-child-education-the-norm/

Gardner, H. (1983). *Frames of mind: The theory of multiple intelligences.* New York, NY: Basic Books.

Geoghan, T. (2017). *Stolen childhoods: End of childhood report 2017.* Fairfield, CT: Save the Children.

Gilbert, I. (2014). *Independent thinking.* Carmarthen, UK: Independent Thinking Press.

Goleman, D. (2005). *Emotional intelligence.* New York, NY: Bantam Books.

Kohn, A. (2014). *Grit: A skeptical look at the latest educational fad.* Retrieved from www.alfiekohn.org/article/grit/

Krovetz, M.L. (2008). *Fostering resilience: Expecting all students to use their minds and hearts well, 2/e.* Thousand Oaks, CA: Corwin Press.

Lopez, A. (2017). *Save the children: U.S. ranks 36 in "end of childhood" index.* Retrieved from http://wshu.org/post/save-children-us-ranks-36-end-childhood-index#stream/0

Masten, A. (2015, June). Resilience in human development: Interdependent adaptive systems in theory and action. Presentation at Pathways to Resilience III, at the University of Minnesota, Minneapolis, MN. Retrieved from http://www.resilienceresearch.org/files/PTR/AnnMasten-PTRKeynote.pdf

Nathan, L.F. (2017). *When grit isn't enough: A high school principal examines how poverty and inequality thwart the college-for-all promise.* Boston, MA: Beacon Press.

Nathan, P., Wallis, H.B., & Hazen, J.H. (Producers), & Hathaway, H. (Director). (1969). *True grit.* Los Angeles, CA: Paramount Pictures.

Rodriguez, V., & Fitzpatrick, M. (2014). *The teaching brain: An evolutionary trait at the heart of education.* New York, NY: The New Press.

Rotter, J. (1954). *Social learning and clinical psychology.* Englewood Cliffs, NJ: Prentice-Hall.

Sultan, A. (2015). When grit isn't enough. *Education Writers Association.* Retrieved from www.ewa.org/blog-educated-reporter/when-grit-isnt-enough

Tough, P. (2012). *How children succeed.* New York, NY: Houghton Mifflin Harcourt Publishing Company.

Wasmuth, H. (2017). Baby PISA is just around the corner: So why is no one talking about it? *ECE PolicyWorks.* Retrieved from http://ecepolicyworks.com/baby-pisa-is-just-around-the-corner-so-why-is-no-one-talking-about-it/

Werner, E.E., & Smith, R.S. (2001). *Journeys from childhood to midlife: Risk, resilience, and recovery.* Ithaca, NY: Cornell University Press.

2

Constructing an Understanding of Grit

What is it about some children that causes or allows them to be so persistent? Teachers and caregivers and coaches and bosses and countless others have used words to help children find the resolve to stick with something, to not give up when the desire to do so is strong: "Today was hard; tomorrow will be better" (Henkes, 1996). The fact is that it doesn't even matter whether or not tomorrow *is* better—they're already in it. Sometimes getting over the hump, and simply moving forward, makes all the difference in whether or not a child completes a social or academic task. Teachers and caregivers have long pondered such questions about persistence and have examined their own styles of teaching and parenting to consider how they might best instill grit—or "gritty" behaviors—in the children with whom they interact, and love.

Some children seem to possess determination and persistence from birth, as character or personality traits, yet other children do not display these qualities, which often appear to be connected to self-esteem, confidence, and motivation. If the qualities are not hardwired in us at birth, then the nature versus nurture theory suggests that these qualities must be connected to something—or *someone*—in the environment. And this is precisely what researchers have suggested as a result of studies conducted over the last 50 years:

> Not every grit paragon has had the benefit of a wise father and mother, but every one I've interviewed could point to *someone* in their life who, at the right time and in the right way,

encouraged them to aim high and provided badly needed confidence and support.

(Duckworth, 2016, pp. 219–220)

This is consistent with Werner and Smith's (2001) findings, discussed
in Chapter 1. One of the elements that research participants cited as
making a difference in their lives, and in their ultimate abilities to succeed in the face of adversity, was the support of one individual in their
lives who became a consistent source of strength and support over
time. As the prominent researcher associated with the concept of grit,
Angela Duckworth (2016) articulates what you have likely already felt
in your work as a teacher of young children: "emerging research on
teaching suggests uncanny parallels to parenting. It seems that psycho-
logically wise teachers can make a huge difference in the lives of their
students" (p. 218). She further credits "wise" teachers as those "who
seem to promote competence in addition to well-being, engagement,
and high hopes for the future" (p. 216). As we examine some of the
definitions and theories related to grit, consider factors and qualities
that matter in the long haul, and the ways that these are reflected—or
not—in a classroom environment.

Definitions and Theories

As mentioned in Chapter 1, the word "grit" typically conjures up asso-
ciations with words such as "tough," "persistence," and "fortitude,"
and there is a clear, consistent bias toward the notion of difficulty that
has been overcome to cross the finish line. Without difficulty, or some
challenge, the successful completion wouldn't be as important or special. To gain a deeper understanding of the word *grit* in all its hardi-
ness, it is helpful to examine some of the vocabulary and the research
connected to these terms that provide the foundation upon which grit
has found a stable platform, and from which it has launched efforts
across distinct disciplines to increase grit in individuals of varying
ages so that they can live more successful lives, however that success
is defined.

First, for the purposes of this writing, *grit* is considered as something that can be developed, and not something one either possesses or
doesn't. Shortly after Hurricane Harvey inflicted devastation in many
parts of Texas, I heard a radio broadcaster speak of the "pluck" that
residents of Houston were showing as they attempted to recover from
the environmental and personal devastation. It struck me then, and I
continue to wrestle with the words that we use to describe behaviors,

that when we make judgments about behaviors, we must also examine the lenses through which we are perceiving their actions and abilities. For example, among any classroom of children, there are likely several children who demonstrate grit in a particular domain, such as games or sports, and other children who display grit in other ways, such as working to finish a puzzle or resolve a conflict with friends. Is the ability to display grit in the wake of a specific, onetime incident different from the ability to endure chronic hardship, such as homelessness or abuse? We may never know, and in the classroom, teachers' lenses are primarily focused on academic outcomes, with social and psychological development often relegated to a secondary, peripheral space. Considering the biological, psychological, and social interplay that contributes to development, it is important to consider the role that strategies play in relation to grit.

Persistence and Delay of Gratification

Persistence is related to six specific strategies (not character traits):

- ◆ Tolerating ambiguity
- ◆ Learning to take moderate risks
- ◆ Acquiring a sense of personal courage
- ◆ Valuing delay of gratification
- ◆ Avoiding rigid thinking
- ◆ Avoiding "drift"

(Dacey, Mack, & Fiore, 2016)

Among these strategies, delay of gratification is often discussed as related to self-control or self-regulation.

These terms have been deemed of high importance for children to succeed academically and to develop "character" (e.g., Tough, 2012). The general understanding among psychologists is that if a child can learn to delay gratification, then subsequent positive outcomes will follow. "The research very clearly shows that people with high self-regulation don't just succeed with their goals, they also enjoy ancillary benefits like greater confidence, more friends, and amplified wellbeing" (Miller, 2017, p. 136).

The Marshmallow Test

What does delay of gratification look like in a classroom context? Researcher and author Ellen Galinsky (2010) describes it as "inhibiting one's initial response to achieve a larger goal" (p. 5), under the broader category of "Focus and Self-Control"—the first essential life skill that every child needs. She notes that this skill involves other strategies, such as "paying attention" and "remembering the rules." In making her case, Galinsky references the well-known "Marshmallow Test," a study conducted by Walter Mischel. In this study, children were given the choice between eating one reward (marshmallow) right away, or waiting for a period of time, after which they would receive a larger reward (two marshmallows). According to Galinsky, this test "has become synonymous with temptation, willpower, and grit" in recent years (p. 5). The reason for this is that a child's ability to wait for the larger reward, while it was more difficult to do so, led to wondering about delay of gratification being a cognitive skill or strategy, similar to a muscle that you can choose to flex or not (Urist, 2014).

The Marshmallow Tests were conducted with children at Stanford University, as well as children in the South Bronx—an area understood to be higher in terms of residents' stress and poverty conditions—and similar findings were revealed in each location. Mischel argued that the Marshmallow Test isn't ultimately about the marshmallows; rather, it's about trust in one's decision-making. Mischel stated:

> [I]n the Marshmallow Tests, the first thing we do is make sure the researcher is someone who is extremely familiar to the child and plays with them in the playroom before the test. It's also important to realize, it's not a matter of if somebody will come back with the two little marshmallows. They are all right there on the tray. It's all out in the open, so there's no trust issue about whether the marshmallows are real.
>
> (Urist, 2014, par. 8)

Recognizing that the main issue for children was not, in fact, whether or not they would have access to the marshmallows, but whether or not they should choose to wait, researchers began to ask questions that could help them understand the relationships between a child's brain and that child's behaviors. For example, how can a child regulate/control herself in ways that make her more successful? Will these decisions/strategies ultimately make her life better? The position shared by Galinsky, Mischel, and psychologist Angela Duckworth is *yes*. Furthermore, these researchers believe that these skills can be taught.

Angela Duckworth

"If children try hard, stay on task, and keep pressing through difficulties, good things happen" (Anders, 2017, par. 1), claims Duckworth, whose book, *Grit: The Power of Passion and Perseverance* (2016) has been touted as the secret to success for children and adults, including NBA and NFL players and business professionals. Duckworth cites qualities such as a "'never give up' attitude" and "this kind of hang-in-there posture toward challenge" (Duckworth, 2016, p. 7). In her extensive research, Duckworth interviewed many people across many domains. Over time, she began to recognize patterns, both in the qualities that people would describe as they recounted stories about individuals who seemed to possess tremendous talent or ability, and in how something happened along the way before these individuals could realize their full potential.

What accounted for the difference? Consistent with ideas that will be discussed in more detail in the following chapter with regard to resilience, it was evident that "[s]ome people are great when things are going well, but they fall apart when things aren't" (Duckworth, 2016, p. 7). People who displayed grit across different fields and domains seemed to possess "a kind of ferocious determinism that played out in two ways. First, these exemplars were unusually resilient and hard-working. Second, they knew in a very, very deep way what it was they wanted. They not only had determination, they had *direction*" (Duckworth, 2016, p. 8).

Talent

To better understand this, Duckworth makes a clear distinction between grit and talent. She uses spelling bee participants as an example to illustrate her ideas. Specifically, when spelling bee participants' performances were examined, those students who studied more hours and participated in more spelling bees went further in the competition. Therefore, Duckworth notes, "potential is one thing. What we do with it is quite another" (Duckworth, 2016, p. 14).

Shifting gears to a different domain, Duckworth describes her own experiences as a middle school math teacher. She notes a distinction between students who performed well based on straightforward talent and those who displayed grit:

> When they didn't get something the first time around, they tried again and again, sometimes coming for extra help during their lunch period or during afternoon electives. Their hard work showed in their grades. Apparently, aptitude did *not* guarantee achievement. Talent for math was different from excelling in math class.
>
> (p. 17)

Duckworth's understanding of grit came into greater clarity when she realized that she had assumed that "those for whom things came easily would continue to outpace their classmates" and that she had been "distracted by talent" (p. 17). She cautions readers that by emphasizing or focusing on talent, we all miss other important factors that contribute to success or lack of achievement. "We inadvertently send the message that these other factors—including grit—don't matter as much as they really do" (p. 31).

Teachers, coaches, and caregivers frequently fall into this trap, categorizing children who possess certain talents for an activity or content area, labeling them as "good" at something or identifying them as "experts" in an area that other children can turn to as resources. The problem isn't giving credit where credit is due when a child excels in a certain area, but rather ignoring the sometimes invisible effort, experience, or training that contributed to *how* someone got to a level of excellence. Others have described the most important aspect of talent in very direct terms, noting the significance of

> working hard, for practicing even when practice isn't fun. It's about putting in the hours when we'd rather be watching TV, or drilling ourselves with notecards filled with obscure words instead of getting quizzed by a friend. Success is never easy. That's why talent requires grit.
>
> (Lehrer, 2011, par. 10)

Practice

So if talent requires grit, then talent is directly related to practice, which requires effort (Lehrer, 2011). But unlike a geometric proof that leads us to conclusions about talent and practice, some factors related to practice raise important questions about access and equity:

> What conditions must be met to allow someone to practice for long? *What is long enough?*
>
> What inclines some people toward practice or toward other pursuits? *What is the role of disposition?*
>
> What is the definition of hard work? *Who decides what is hard enough? Is this measurable?*

As will be discussed in more detail later in this chapter, Duckworth anchors her work squarely in the field of psychology, and therefore focuses her arguments about grit in the cognitive domain, where the boundaries of access and equity are less clearly identifiable. For example, a child in a family with resources to pay for piano lessons can more readily practice piano than a child who cannot afford piano lessons, or has never played or heard live piano music. For teachers who typically consider universal access and multiple entry points into a curriculum when designing classroom experiences for all learners, it requires some suspension of disbelief to focus on the role of practice without questioning equity.

Eyes on the Prize

For the purposes of discussion, and assuming relatively equal access for all students, elements of deliberate, intentional practice include:

◆   A clearly defined stretch goal
◆   Full concentration and effort
◆   Immediate and informative feedback
◆   Repetition with reflection and refinement

(Duckworth, 2016, p. 137)

Building on the concept of persistence, grit is more than stubborn adherence to a plan or goal. It's also about identifying the right goal from the beginning (Groth, 2012). In a recent interview, author Jonah Lehrer noted that "[t]he only ideas worth pursuing are those you'd be willing to invest 10,000 hours into" (Groth, 2012). Lehrer's words echo psychologist Mihaly Csikszentmihalyi's same ideas about talent and practice—that to make a significant difference in outcome or ability takes about 10,000 hours of practice, and the practice itself can, at times, be extremely boring and even unpleasant. The distinction, Csikszentmihalyi (2014) argues, is that "when the learning is hard, it is not bitter when you feel that it is worth having" (p. xx).

Even the goal of attempting to explain this thing called grit is, in itself, gritty. Duckworth acknowledges that her work contributes to a canon of psychological theories that attempt to explain the human condition. In her book, she describes her own realization that her theory is an explanation, and like all theories is therefore an oversimplification. While her theory may help readers better understand talent and achievement, there is always room for more questions, as well as challenges to assumptions. Perhaps most relevant to teachers of young children is the following assertion:

Talent is how quickly your skills improve when you invest effort. Achievement is what happens when you take your acquired skills and use them. Of course, your opportunities—for example, having a great coach or teacher—matter tremendously, too, and maybe more than anything about the individual. My theory doesn't address these outside forces, nor does it include luck. It's about the psychology of achievement, but because psychology isn't all that matters, it's incomplete.

(Duckworth, 2016, p. 42)

And because all theory invites questions and critique, and because Duckworth's acknowledgement of the narrow lens through which she examined grit opened the door for consideration of grit's fit in other domains, we turn now to an alternative perspective—from author and educator Alfie Kohn.

Alfie Kohn

In his direct and unequivocal manner, Kohn (2014) argues that "Duckworth is *selling* grit, not dispassionately investigating its effects" (par. 6). Kohn—a longtime advocate of children's learning and of educators' rights to teach according to best practices, not mandates of the moment—warns readers that the concept of *grit* is a fad. He argues that the problem with educational fads is that they tend to spark energy and educational practices that are ultimately detrimental to children's learning. For example, in response to the notion of identifying an appropriate goal, he warns that when educators focus on learning as a measure of grit, the goal becomes "to make sure kids will resist temptation, override their unconstructive impulses, put off doing what they enjoy in order to grind through whatever they've been told to do—and keep at it for as long as it takes" (Kohn, 2014, par. 3).

Whereas Duckworth (2016) extols the ability of people to focus on the same top-level goal for extended periods of time, incorporating mid-level and low-level goals that are, in some way or another, related to the ultimate goal, Kohn posits that "not everything is *worth* doing, let alone doing for extended periods" (par. 8). He further states, "The amorality of the concept enables the immorality of some individuals who exemplify it. This would be a better world if people who were up to no good had *less* grit" (par. 8).

At a time when teachers of young children often find themselves conflicted, weighing their loyalties to children and what they know to be true about child development against their duties as paid teaching staff who are held accountable to the scores that their students or their schools receive on standardized measures, Kohn's self-proclaimed skepticism provides an important perspective. When Duckworth argues that "the more unified, aligned, and coordinated our goal hierarchies, the better" (Duckworth, 2016, p. 66), it is important to consider the social and cultural factors that influence the values that contribute to these goals in the first place.

Social and Cultural Issues That Influence the Development of Grit

What follows are excerpts from writing about several famous individuals—people who represent grit at different ages, for different reasons, and at different geographical places and times over the course of history. As you read the excerpts, consider what you would underline or highlight as evidence of grit, and what values are reflected in those specific items.

On Ruby Bridges

When Ruby got inside the building, she was all alone except for her teacher, Miss Hurley. There were no other children to keep Ruby company, to play with and learn with, to eat lunch with. But every day, Ruby went into the classroom with a big smile on her face, ready to get down to the business of learning.

(Coles, 1995)

On Sojourner Truth

Sojourner's voice was packed with power. As she traveled, she learned even more about the meaning of freedom. She found that freedom is not a place. Freedom is the fire that burns inside. And Sojourner Truth, she was full of fire. Once, when Sojourner was scheduled to speak at a rally, someone threatened to burn down the building. That didn't stop Sojourner. She said, "I will speak upon its ashes."

(Pinkney, 2009)

No other woman who had been through the ordeal of slavery managed to survive with sufficient strength, poise, and self-confidence to become a public presence over the long term. . . . Only Truth had the ability to go on speaking, year after year for thirty years, to make herself into a force in several American reform movements.

(Painter, 1996, p. 4)

On Gandhi

> "Select your purpose," he challenged, "selfless, without any thought of personal pleasure or personal profit, and then use selfless means to attain your goal. Do not resort to violence even if it seems at first to promise success; it can only contradict your purpose. Use the means of love and respect even if the result seems far off or uncertain. Then throw yourself heart and soul into the campaign, counting no price too high for working for the welfare of those around you, and every reverse, every defeat, will send you deeper into your own deepest resources."
>
> (Easwaran, 2011, p. 69)

After reading descriptions of these three individuals, what elements can you identify that are common to each of them and their situations? How does this enhance your understanding of grit?

Duckworth (2016) suggests that a critical element is the notion of purpose—"the idea that what we do matters to people other than ourselves" (p. 145). Perhaps this is one element that struck you as you read the passages above. Each of these individuals acted to bring about change for others, at great personal risk to themselves. The risks they were vulnerable to included physical risks as well as emotional harm. It is interesting to consider what elements of a particular society or context inhibit or support risk-taking. Does an individual's culture of origin frown upon individual risk-taking? Is the safety and well-being of the group more important than that of one individual, and how does this contribute to one's sense of purpose?

Each of the individuals described in the passages above also acted in spite of fear. Researchers who have examined fear and courage have noted the role that fear has in both inhibiting and strengthening our resolve. "Fear is not our enemy. We don't need to get rid of fear or push it away. We need to learn how to be afraid" (Clark, 2011, p. 16). Author Taylor Clark notes the different uses of the word "nerve" in relation to fear, stating, "Having 'a case of nerves' is a common synonym for fear itself, yet 'showing nerve' signifies moral courage" (p. 16). Clark explains that the emotional states of "fear and cool" share more commonalities than we might imagine, and that these two emotions are even necessary for each other to function:

> Our anxieties never need to be our enemies; indeed, some of the most neurotic and fearful people on the planet are also

the iciest customers under fire. What truly separates the cool-headed from the hotheads in tense times isn't *whether* they feel fear—which is largely beyond their conscious control—but how they *relate* to their fear.

(p. 50)

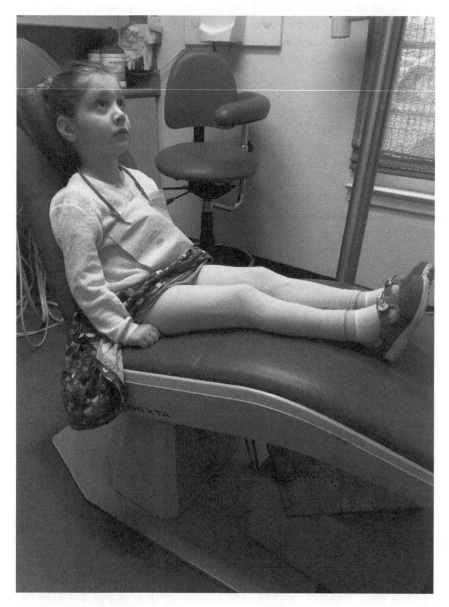

Figure 2.1 At the Dentist

Just as we often never see all of the hours of effort and practice that an individual navigates when they perform well in spite of difficult outcomes, and thus display grit:

> When we see heroic, cool-headed characters coming through under stress, delivering sound decisions and performing smoothly, we often see their poise as primarily the product of innate character. . . . But though disposition does play a role, it's only one side of the story. . . . What you're unable to see is this huge iceberg under the water that constitutes all of the experience and practice and thought that has been put into how to deal with that stress.'. . . Only arduous, plentiful experience can give you the rock-solid instincts you need to make good decisions under fire.
>
> (Clark, 2011, pp. 122–123)

As teachers consider the benefits of managing fear for students whose dispositions or families influence their understanding of "success," they can also imagine ways that classroom environments diminish or harness fear. The activities in this chapter help children identify goals and opportunities in order to nurture their curiosity and well-being.

Effects of Heredity and the Environment

It's a challenging task for teachers to consider the different attitudes and aptitudes of all of the unique individuals who learn together in a classroom environment. Each child brings with her the biological, psychological, and social traits that are either inherited or learned, sometimes influenced by a combination of the two. While there is some obvious value in remembering personal experiences with grit, even more valuable is the ability to learn from and remember the experiences of others. Gardner (2008) explains:

> After all, there's only one of you. But when you sit around the campfire after a long day of foraging, there may be twenty or thirty other people. If you can gather their experiences, you will multiply the information on which your judgments are based twenty or thirty times.
>
> (p. 50)

Duckworth (2016) addresses the question of whether we inherit grit from our DNA by suggesting that there is both a short answer and a long one. "The short answer is 'in part.' The long answer is . . . more compli-cated" and includes "genes, experience, and their interplay" (p. 79).

For example, time and experience play a role. Even if we could argue that personality is something that is inherited and biological, the way one's personality changes over time is the result of life expe-rience. Even if we could argue that personality is fixed and remains stable over time, the circumstances that someone experiences change over time. Duckworth posits that as people develop over time, they are presented with new situations. "And, because there's no species on the planet more adaptable than ours, we change. We rise to the occasion" (p. 87).

To illustrate the inherited and environmental influences on grit, Duckworth presents an example from Finland, and the Finnish peo-ple, specifically—the word *sisu* [pronounced see-sue]. Noting that this word more accurately reflects perseverance than passion, she explains that

> *sisu* refers to a source of inner strength—a sort of psychologi-cal capital—that the Finns believe they're born with by dint of their Finnish heritage. Quite literally, *sisu* refers to the insides of a person, their guts.
>
> (p. 250)

As soon as I read this passage, I contacted a dear friend of mine—a woman born in Finland who has lived in several cities in Canada and the United States, and recently moved to Mauritius, an African country located in the Indian Ocean. As it happens, she has a 9-year-old dog named Sisu, and I asked her if she purposely chose that name with the Finnish connotation in mind.

She then shared a remarkable story with me. On a recent business trip to Rwanda—where she stays one week each month—her dog Sisu had been attacked by a local Rwandan dog. Sisu had managed to escape the grip of the Rwandan dog's jaws, wriggling out of his leash in the process, and bolting away from the scene. My friend searched frantically for Sisu, to no avail, and spent a tortured night worrying that Sisu was badly injured, or worse. The next day, Sisu found his way home, limping and bruised, but otherwise intact. I couldn't believe the courage and tenacity that Sisu had demonstrated, or the timing of this experience. And it raised a new question for me about the impact that grit can have on an individual—regardless of species: how much of grit is intuitive and how much is the result of learning?

The Role of the Brain

From an evolutionary perspective, humans have developed the capacity to defend ourselves and spring into action when faced with obstacles or threats—real or perceived. The well-known fight-or-flight response is pre-wired into each one of us, and it is activated in a specific part of the human brain—a small, almond-shaped region (one located in each hemisphere) called the amygdala. When the brain receives distress signals, this triggers the release of hormones from the amygdala, including adrenaline and cortisol. Some of the physical symptoms of this response include an increased heart rate, dilation of pupils, and muscle tension, often in the head, neck, shoulders, and stomach.

Although the fight-or-flight response is intended to initiate a quick reaction to immediate threats, researchers have noted one feature intended to have a long-lasting effect. Specifically, the hormones that the amygdala triggers temporarily enhance memory function, so the experience that prompted the fight-or-flight response "will be vividly encoded and remembered" (Gardner, 2008, p. 49). So perhaps an argument can be made for an elegant blueprint of human design that considered the mutual influence of biology and experience.

The Role of Learning

Can experience influence biology? Some researchers propose that over time, through repetition and experience, people can train themselves to do what they consider to be the desirable or "right" thing (Clark, 2011). This resonates with supporters of rote memorization and is consistent with the emphasis that Duckworth places on practice, in that practice with any given skill or task is the most reliable way to ensure success.

Yet some memorization occurs at an unconscious level. For example, neuroscientists have studied the amygdalae of people sitting in a quiet, safe university laboratory setting. Their research has shown that participants' amygdalae are activated when frightening or threatening images are shown for a fleeting fraction of a second—such a brief amount of time that people aren't even able to recall the face as expressing fear or distress. In fact, they most often describe the faces as "expressionless." Yet the activation of the amygdala and the subsequent hormone release "makes the memory more vivid, lasting, and recallable" (Gardner, 2008, p. 49).

How then, do teachers reconcile what may be a fleeting association with the long-term, disciplined concept known as grit?

Implications and Inspiration

An argument can be made that the purpose of instilling grit in young children is to encourage them to persist along their paths toward clear and measurable goals. The underlying idea is that this will ultimately enhance their academic achievement. However, an argument can also be made for the benefits of knowing when *not* to persist, which will ultimately benefit other areas of their being—some measurable, and some perhaps not—not excluding academic achievement.

Kohn (2014) cautions teachers and caregivers that a focus *only* on measurable behaviors won't provide critical information about whether a student who displays grit demonstrates persistence because of a deep and inspiring love of the activity, or because of a desperate need to please an authority figure and prove her competence (Kohn, 2014). While Duckworth's (2016) research relies primarily on measurable behaviors and outcomes, she summarizes the elements that combine to create grit as follows:

> First comes *interest*. . . . Next comes the capacity to *practice*. One form of perseverance is the daily discipline of trying to do things better than we did yesterday. . . . Third is *purpose*. What ripens passion is the conviction that your work matters. . . . And finally, *hope*.
>
> (p. 91)

In the quote that opened this chapter, Lilly's classroom teacher, Mr. Slinger, encouraged Lilly to persist, promising that *tomorrow will be better*. It is precisely this relationship between teacher and student that presents opportunities for success on multiple levels.

So how or why do some people get up when they've been knocked down or unsuccessful, not once, but sometimes over and over again? In the chapter that follows, the concept of resilience is examined as it contributes to a deeper understanding of children's development in a complex developmental context.

Turning Ideas Into Action

Dream Boards
Goal: To identify a goal or hope that provides a sense of purpose, even if this changes over time

Materials needed: Poster board, size 11″ x 14″; magazines to rip or cut images from; scissors; glue or glue sticks; crayons or markers

Action: This activity may be used as a one-on-one or small group activity. If working with a group, it will be important to pay attention to the dynamic between children and their respective comfort levels sharing ideas. Ask the child(ren) to think about something that they want or hope to achieve. What does this look like? Ask the child(ren) to close their eyes and see this idea in their minds. What does this look like? Invite children to look through magazines and find images that resonate with or reflect their ideas about their goal(s). Using their hands or scissors, they can rip or cut the images from magazines and glue them onto their boards. Ask children to share with each other what is displayed on their boards. Is there significance to the placement of different images in proximity to the other, for example? Are some images concrete while others are abstract? Place these boards in the classroom where children can easily view them and reflect upon them. Encourage the children to check in with each other about their boards, asking each other if they have made progress toward their goal(s). Can they point to an image that reflects this progress? As children visualize their goals, they are more able to notice the progress toward these goals as well as obstacles along the way.

Interview a Grown-up

Goal: To learn about others' experiences, including how they worked hard toward a long-term goal

Materials needed: None, though a camera can be useful to take pictures of individuals who share their stories so that children may revisit these ideas at a future time. You may want paper/a pencil for your own notetaking.

Action: Invite children's family members or other community members into the classroom to share their stories of perseverance. If you have a sense of what the individual will share in advance, brainstorm with the children some questions they would like to ask. For example, "Did you ever feel like giving up or stopping? What did you do when you felt that way?" or "Was there someone that you talked to when you needed help? Who was it and how did they help?" are some questions that will stimulate conversation. As the conversation evolves, make note of the questions children ask, and as time passes during the school year, you can remind them of the conversation as applicable to encourage them toward their own goals.

Turn Your Whoops Into Wow!

Goal: To learn how mistakes or outcomes that seem undesirable can turn into opportunities

Materials needed: Bulletin board or wall area dedicated to this topic; camera to capture "whoops!" and "wow!" moments; art materials (e.g., paper, paints, brushes, crayons, markers, scissors)

Figure 2.2 Celebration Collage

Action: Explain to children that sometime we start with one idea or plan, and then something happens—"Whoops!" We might make a mistake, or we forget something, or someone tells us something that makes us feel less sure of our idea. How can we look at mistakes differently and see them as invitations to create something new?

Begin with an example of artwork, such as that of Jackson Pollock (e.g., *No.1 Lavender Mist*), which at first may look messy or confusing to children, since it's not a concrete representation of an object or scene. See what children notice about the art, such as texture, lines, and splatters, and then invite children to create their own artwork in the spirit of Pollock's "action" painting style.

Alternatively, provide children with magazines and newspapers and invite them to rip images and words from the pages and then use them to create collages from these images. Children may use the magazine images to create texture and depth that a two-dimensional process typically does not afford. (Note: throughout this book, the collage artwork created by 10-year-old Ellis Grace Brown is included to inspire readers and children with whom they work, as well as to represent and celebrate the talent and creativity that young children possess that is all too often overlooked by adults.)

Encourage children to provide feedback to other children using the prompts, "I really like how you . . ." and "Your artwork made me think about ____ in a different way." These simple statements reinforce process and effort, validating children's instincts and choices.

A Closer Look: Children's Behavior Through the "Grit" Lens

Asiya established her reputation for being "determined" two years ago, when she started in the Toddler Two classroom at the center. One of her mother's favorite examples to share with others was that after only three days at the center, and as one of the younger children in the class, Asiya chose to use the toilet like most of the students rather than wear diapers or Pull-Ups. Her mother had been delighted! She always laughed as she told the story, remembering that Asiya had never expressed *any* interest or desire to use the potty before that day, and even rewards like coins she could put into her piggy bank had been only moderately successful. But Asiya's determination to be like her peers was strong, and "once she sets her mind on a goal, that's that!"

Asiya's teacher, Miss Leah, had known the family since Asiya's older brother Ismael was a student in the same preschool class two years ago. She'd heard about, and then witnessed first-hand, Asiya's determination. She enjoyed challenging Asiya to be patient and manage frustration if she encountered a task that she couldn't master right away. Miss Leah noted, smiling, that this didn't happen often, as Asiya tended to tackle tasks until she was able to complete them.

"It's almost like she's driven to complete them," explained Miss Leah. "It's not so much about competition as it is about mastery. She doesn't need to be offered rewards, although who doesn't like rewards now and then? It's like she's got some inner coach pushing her forward. All I know is, if I'm ever on *Survivor*, I want her on *my* team!"

***

One sunny morning in May, Asiya burst into the preschool classroom and declared to Miss Leah, "I'm going to get a *library* card! Mama said that I can get one like Ismael as soon as I can write my name. That's the rules!"

"You're going to get a *library* card? That's fantastic! I didn't know you can write your name already!" Miss Leah looked at Asiya's mother and smiled. Mrs. Bousaid raised her hands in an "I give up!" gesture, and smiled back.

"We're working on it," Mrs. Bousaid said warmly, patting Asiya's head as she hurried to transfer her belongings from her tote bag to her cubby.

"Can I go to the writing table to practice my letters?" Asiya asked excitedly.

Miss Leah told her, "Of course! I'll come over to help you in a moment. I'll just say hello to Mom."

Mrs. Bousaid told Miss Leah that Ismael had gotten his first library card on Saturday and had proudly checked out his books by himself. The idea that one could have one's own card (in its own shiny plastic card holder no less!) had captivated Asiya for the rest of the weekend. The family had played with letter blocks and Mrs. Bousaid had written out Asiya's name for her to copy, which she had tried to do several times, with some small success. Miss Leah assured Mrs. Bousaid that they would help Asiya practice as much as she'd like, to help her reach her goal.

***

During naptime, Miss Leah made a photocopy of her own library card and then used correction fluid to hide her own handwriting. She then made subsequent copies of the blank library card template, which she planned to put out on the writing table as models that Asiya and other children could use as practice templates once they could write the letters that spelled out their names.

Miss Leah also created practice sheets with lines for children to use, practicing writing their names, in sequentially smaller sizes:

1. _____
   _____
   _____
2. _____
   _____
3. _____
   _____

She presented these sheets of paper on the writing table along with writing tools of various kinds—pencils, markers, crayons, chalk, oil pastels, and charcoal. During choice time, several children spent time at the table, practicing writing their first and last names. Asiya spent over 30 minutes at the writing table, happily writing her letters over and over again, and accepting help from Miss Leah to make her letters "stand up taller" and "look like teacher writing." At the end of the school day, Miss Leah gave Asiya some papers to continue practicing at home.

***

On Thursday morning, Asiya trotted into the classroom and threw her arms around Miss Leah's waist.

"Guess what I gahh-ahht!" she sang.

"Hmmm . . . could it be something that you've been working on in school?" asked Miss Leah.

"You KNOW it is!" Asiya cheered. "I got my own *libary* card!" Asiya thrust her plastic card case in front of Miss Leah, who took it gingerly, as if it were a delicate, precious item.

"Wow, Asiya! That's wonderful! You got your own *library* card! You must feel very proud of all your hard work." She smiled at Asiya.

"I know! And now I can check out books on my own and Mama and Papa don't even have to know which ones I take because of

Figure 2.3 Library Card

privacy! The *libary* lady told me those are rules. But I will always show them because they READ to me, silly!" Asiya skipped away to show her friend Iliana her new prized possession.

"When did she become a *teenager*?" Miss Leah asked Mrs. Bousaid.

"Easy, now—I'm not sure I'm quite ready for that!" Mrs. Bousaid laughed. "Let's see what today brings first."

Resources

The Grit Scale

http://angeladuckworth.com/grit-scale/

This website features the 10-item Grit Scale developed by Angela Duckworth. Upon completing this survey, the individual receives a "grit score" and may follow prompts to learn more about grit and the research that informed Dr. Duckworth's book and continued work.

SEAD—The ASPEN Institute

www.aspeninstitute.org/tag/sead/

The National Commission on Social, Emotional, and Academic Development (AspenSEAD) explores how social-emotional learning can be integrated into educational settings to support children's overall growth and development. It recognizes that every child brings their own personal experience to the learning process, and the goal is for every child to receive the supports they need to succeed in school, in the workplace, and over the course of their lifetimes.

Zero to Three

www.zerotothree.org

This organization works to ensure that children receive the developmental supports that will contribute to their lifelong health and well-being. Resources for children, caregivers, and practitioners are provided, underscoring the belief that early connections and meaningful experiences have a lasting impact.

References

Anders, G. (2017). Can grit be measured? Angela Duckworth is working on it. *EdSurge*. Retrieved from www.edsurge.com/news/2017-03-27-can-grit-be-measured-angela-duckworth-is-working-on-it

Clark, T. (2011). *Nerve: Poise under pressure, serenity under stress, and the brave new science of fear and cool.* New York, NY: Little, Brown and Company.

Coles, R. (1995). *The story of Ruby Bridges.* New York, NY: Scholastic.

Csikszentmihalyi, M. (2014). *Applications of flow in human development: The collected works of Mihaly Csikszentmihalyi.* Dordrecht, Netherlands: Springer.

Dacey, J.S., Mack, M.D., & Fiore, L.B. (2016). *Your anxious child: How parents and teachers can relieve anxiety in children, 2/e.* Oxford, UK: John Wiley & Sons.

Duckworth, A. (2016). *Grit: The power of passion and perseverance.* New York, NY: Scribner.

Easwaran, E. (2011). *Gandhi the man: How one man changed himself to change the world.* Tomales, CA: Nilgiri Press.

Galinsky, E. (2010). *Mind in the making: The seven essential life skills every child needs.* New York, NY: HarperCollins Publishers.

Gardner, D. (2008). *The science of fear: Why we fear the things we shouldn't- and put ourselves in greater danger.* New York, NY: Dutton.

Groth, A. (2012). If your idea doesn't pass the "underwear test", you probably won't be successful. *Business Insider.* Retrieved from www.businessinsider.com/if-your-idea-doesnt-pass-the-underwear-test-you-probably-wont-be-successful-2012-5

Henkes, K. (1996). *Lilly's purple plastic purse.* New York, NY: Greenwillow Books.

Kohn, A. (2014). *Grit: A skeptical look at the latest educational fad.* Retrieved from www.alfiekohn.org/article/grit/

Lehrer, J. (2011). Which traits predict success? (The importance of grit). *Wired.* Retrieved from www.wired.com/2011/03/what-is-success-true-grit/

Miller, C.A. (2017). *Getting grit: The evidence-based approach to cultivating passion, perseverance, and purpose.* Boulder, CO: Sounds True.

Painter, N.I. (1996). *Sojourner Truth: A life, a symbol.* New York, NY: W.W. Norton & Company, Inc.

Pinkney, A.D. (2009). *Sojourner Truth's step-stomp stride.* New York, NY: Disney Jump at the Sun Books.

Tough, P. (2012). *How children succeed.* New York, NY: Houghton Mifflin Harcourt Publishing Company.

Urist, J. (2014). What the marshmallow test really teaches about self-control. *The Atlantic.* Retrieved from www.theatlantic.com/health/archive/2014/09/what-the-marshmallow-test-really-teaches-about-self-control/380673/

Werner, E.E., & Smith, R.S. (2001). *Journeys from childhood to midlife: Risk, resilience, & recovery.* Ithaca, NY: Cornell University Press.

3

Constructing an Understanding of Resilience

On the most basic level, the concept of *resilience* is understood to be the ability an individual possesses to bounce back from exposure to adverse risks or experiences. For children, this might look like the ability to endure teasing or mean-spirited behavior from classmates, as protagonist Auggie experiences in R.J. Palacio's (2012) book *Wonder*, or choosing to place one's trust in a teacher who will keep them safe when the adults in their home environments aren't consistently present or reliable. Over the course of a lifetime, adults gain the benefits of lived experiences from which we learn that the world keeps on turning in spite of our academic or social mistakes, and we therefore become increasingly comfortable taking moderate risks and opening ourselves up to new experiences and vulnerability. It is through taking such risks and building a foundation from which to reflect that children learn to analyze situations, develop appropriate responses, and trust their instincts. With practice, children develop this perspective and accompanying skills—to trust their own judgments, think independently, and lead as well as follow. Children are protagonists as they participate in their own life stories.

Definitions and Theories

The concept of resilience has been discussed extensively in research literature, both as something that children possess or demonstrate, and also as something that defines them. The foundational research of Werner and Smith (2001) presented protective factors that, they argued, impact successful human development. These factors included educational milestones, supportive role models, a balance between structure and rules (for males, specifically) and moderate risk-taking and independence (for females, specifically), faith that life would work itself out (not necessarily linked to religious beliefs or observance), responsibility for others, and goal-setting. The researchers began following the lives of 614 children, all born in 1955 on the island of Kauai. The majority of the children were born without any complications. Yet one-third of the children experienced multiple, concurrent risk factors before their second birthday. Within this group of approximately 200 children, two-thirds of the children developed later "problems" (e.g., learning challenges, behavioral issues, juvenile delinquency, teen pregnancy, substance abuse). What became apparent and sparked further investigation is the fact that the remaining third of the children who had experienced multiple risk factors developed into "competent, confident, and caring young adults by age eighteen" (Krovetz, 2008, p. 8). This chapter will identify and explore some of the influences on children's developing resilience in the early childhood years.

For example, recent research has presented resilience as a set of interconnected, interdependent systems in an individual's life, and not solely a trait that one possesses to a specific degree. Ann Masten (2015) created a graphic that illustrates the complexities of resilience (see Figure 3.1). This graphic also reflects the work of respected experts in the field of psychology, such as Urie Bronfenbrenner and Richard Lerner, who proposed the simultaneous, complex influences of numerous systems on a child's development.

Whereas early work on resilience was concerned with the individual, and recent research has considered resilience as a feature of whole communities (e.g., Fleming & Ledogar, 2008), it is interesting to consider how a classroom might embody features of a resilient community, and how teachers are active participants in this system/process.

Krovetz (2008) proposes a definition for a resilient community as one that is "focused on the protective factors that foster resilience for its members: (1) caring, (2), high expectations and purposeful support, and (3) ongoing opportunities for meaningful participation" (p. 2). These elements seem well suited to a classroom context, and early childhood classrooms in particular. Early childhood educators tend to possess and demonstrate high levels of caring, for the simple reason that young children are typically more vulnerable in terms of human

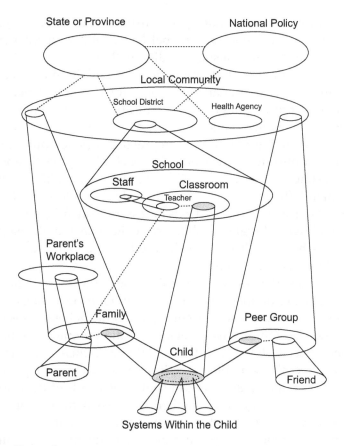

Figure 3.1 Masten Systems

development than are older children. They require care as they work toward developmental goals and milestones, and teachers work to provide academic and social experiences in the curriculum that support such development.

Because early childhood educators work as part of a system that is affected by local, state, and federal values and mandates, it is interesting to consider resilience in an even broader context. For example, what are the effects of community and culture on resilience in individuals? How is resilience manifest** as a feature of entire communities and cultural groups, or among cultural groups within communities? It makes sense that different contexts elicit and support resilience as well as inhibit the development of resilient behaviors. Such complexities have contributed to the notion that resilience is not so much a fixed quality as a process that changes over time (Fleming & Ledogar, 2008).

Expanding the viewfinder even further, Masten has suggested consideration of resilience at a global level, calling for international efforts to promote and sustain resilience (Masten, 2014). As noted in Chapter 1, economic and academic competition on a global scale directly impacts educational experiences for children at every level of schooling—preK through higher education. Masten suggests that "[e]ngaged developmental scientists are not only good for developmental science and its applications in practice or policy, but ultimately important for improving the well-being of children globally and, with these investments, the future well-being of global health and human development" (Masten, 2014, p. 16). In order to understand the resilience process in a global context, it is necessary to identify and evaluate the factors involved that contribute to a child's healthy development, and success however it is defined, based on the values of a specific context at a given point in time.

Where does this leave early childhood educators? It brings us back to the stance of honoring children as unique individuals possessing different strengths and presenting different challenges inside and outside the classroom. This proactive position emphasizes building skills and capacity for all children—building resilience. While teachers cannot "fix" every problem, nor impact every child's experience to the extent we might desire, we can control elements of the classroom environment and work to strengthen the classroom environment as a collaborative act. Researchers underscore this stance, noting that "being proactive means impacting the environment, not defining the child" (Krovetz, 2008, p. 7).

Werner and Smith (2001, p. 172) describe resilience as a "chain of protective factors" that enabled many participants in their research studies to overcome numerous adversities in their early years. According to their findings, these factors functioned as links in the chain. These links included participants' biological makeup (e.g., an intact central nervous system and good health), psychological dispositions (e.g., cognitive skills, temperament, and sense of self-efficacy), and the sources of support (e.g., emotional, economic) they could count on at every stage of development (Werner & Smith, 2001, p. 172). As emphasized in Chapter 1, simply experiencing challenges is not the key to successful development:

> . . . fear does not automatically lead to courage. Injury does not necessarily lead to insight. Hardship will not automatically make us better. Pain can break us or make us wiser. Suffering

can destroy us or make us stronger. Fear can cripple us, or it can make us more courageous. It is resilience that makes the difference.

(Greitens, 2015, pp. 3–4)

There are various biological, psychological, and social factors that interact to influence children's inclinations.

Dandelions and Orchids

For example, in the biological realm, recent research has identified two categories of children—dandelion and orchid children. Boyce and Ellis (2005) describe dandelion children, who "have the capacity to survive—even thrive—in whatever circumstances they encounter," and orchid children, who are extremely sensitive to their environments, and therefore "wither" if neglected but "flourish" if they are nurtured well (Herbert, 2011). It was the delicacy and sensitive nature of the orchid children that led Boyce and Ellis to look beyond environmental issues to genetic components. A specific gene—the CHRM2 gene—has previously been identified in research related to alcohol dependence and serious depression. In the case of resilience, the CHRM2 gene is now considered to interact with enzymes in the body and chemical receptors in the brain, resulting in positive or negative outcomes for children.

This understanding is evident in Tupac Shakur's (1999) poem "The Rose That Grew from Concrete":

Did u hear about the rose that grew from a crack
in the concrete
Proving nature's laws wrong it learned 2 walk
without having feet

(p. 3)

It is curious, and important to notice, that the biological is so often considered as separate from the psychological and social realms, when it is almost impossible to do so with fidelity to human development as a complex, interconnected process. For example, there is a fundamental sense of belonging that has long been argued by theorists (Maslow, 1954) as vital to healthy and successful development. Belongingness is reflected in a child's general trust in others, in her comfort in being similar as well as different from peers, and in a perceived hierarchy in her relationships. As she develops, her social group exerts more influence than parents.

Figure 3.2 Rose Collage

A child's resilience and overall development is also impacted by an environment that includes home and school. Author Edward De Bono (1993) writes:

> If you believe that school is the right place to teach thinking and that schools are doing this well, [this] book is not for you. In my experience, schools do not teach thinking at all. Some schools teach the limited thinking skills involved in information sorting and analysis.
>
> (p. 3)

This tends to be the focus of most school curricula, as opposed to encouraging children to reread and rewrite the world (Freire, 2000). Supporting children's resilience means encouraging them to celebrate their ideas, even if those ideas are different from those of others (especially yours!), and to be a keen observer of the world. Painters, poets, and most 4-year-olds possess the ability to interpret the world as it really is, and the desire to express the results of thoughtful, complex, often unbridled exploration.

Masten proposes that "[t]he resilience of an individual over the course of development depends on the function of complex adaptive systems that are continually interacting and transforming" (Masten, 2014, p. 9). Others (e.g., Luthar, Cicchetti, & Becker, 2000) have identified resilience as a construct with two distinct dimensions: significant adversity and positive adaptation. From this perspective, resilience is never directly measured but is directly inferred from evidence of these dimensions (Fleming & Ledogar, 2008, p. 8). Researchers tend to agree on the notions of adversity and adaptation. In other words, an individual is exposed to some sort of threat or experiences adversity/hardship, and then that individual overcomes this through a process of positive adaptation (Luthar, Cicchetti, & Becker, 2000; Werner & Smith, 2001).

Turning Risk Into Resilience

Some researchers question whether a child's resilience is the result of awareness or actions, and whether or not these qualities can be separated from each other. For example, Werner's (1995) work is cited as identifying three specific variations: positive developmental outcomes in spite of "high-risk" status; evidence of competence while under stress; and recovery from traumatic experiences (Fleming & Ledogar, 2008). Since the majority of children's daily cognitive and social experiences often occur in the context of school, thoughtful critics of the current world climate identify independent thinking as a quality of utmost importance if we want to nurture a society that is creative, collaborative, and resilient.

The ability to think for oneself, to be perceived as different from the crowd, even if it's as simple as pointing up when everyone points down, involves taking risks. The work of Werner and Smith (2001) supports the idea that given the right combination of factors, children can move from being "at-risk" to children who know how to take moderate risks that can actually enhance their present and future development. One of the keys to this transition is to provide young children with opportunities to practice and improve their own problem-solving skills. The activities at the end of this chapter encourage children to develop comfort with exploring new situations through a different lens, and to practice feeling comfortable with the uncertainty that often precedes creative problem-solving.

As children become more comfortable taking moderate risks and trusting their own ideas, they will be better able to evaluate the world around them with confidence and integrity. This is due to the ability to soften self-judgment and the need to be correct, and to appreciate the value of being creative and constructive, and—sometimes—wrong! In order for a child to develop the self-confidence and self-esteem needed for resilient development, she must be able to generate a number of ideas from which to choose and explore.

Independent Thinking and Autonomy

Most teachers would agree that if a child's brain "works" well, then she has a better chance of making informed, safe decisions. It follows that if a child's brain is not operating well, then she might make less ideal, and potentially harmful, decisions. As stated earlier in this chapter, numerous factors contribute to children's resilience and the same may be said of children's thinking. It has therefore been suggested that

> what we think of as free will is largely an illusion: much of the time, we are simply operating on automatic pilot, and the way we think and act—and how well we think and act on the spur of the moment—are a lot more susceptible to outside influences than we realize.
>
> (Gladwell, 2005, p. 58)

Some of these outside influences have a strong impact on our judgments, whether it is how much a child admires the color of another child's shoes, or what box an older student checks off on a standardized text next to a prompt for "race/ethnicity." Researchers have noted this "mental contamination" (Gladwell, 2005; Greenfield, 2011; Marcus, 2008) as often harmless (e.g., marketing campaigns), but often damaging (e.g., lower self-esteem). Therefore, a goal for promoting resilience is to encourage a child to think independently *and* appreciate the multiple perspectives that help inform her thinking. The activities at the end of this chapter encourage your child to think about ideas that no one else is thinking. If we want children to think like everyone else, then there is no need to think "outside the box." If we want children to experiment with new ideas, then they need to develop strategies that challenge and extend what is expected or predictable.

As children develop, they encounter people, traditions, and stories that provide answers to many questions in numerous areas. These explanations may be shared and codified formally, as in a school setting, or informally, from sibling to sibling or friend to friend. Encouraging children to question or examine these accepted "truths"—turning the "what is" upside down—allows children to imagine alternatives. This type of thinking is helpful as children develop their own abilities to think independently and not accept something as truth without examining it from many angles.

There are times when, as a result of weighing multiple perspectives and considering paths of action, children realize that a decision may not be popular or pleasant but will have a better long-term outcome (this will be discussed further in Chapter 4). Similarly, there are times when a child does not have time to weigh her options, but must instead act quickly and trust her instincts. When children find themselves in this situation, it helps if they believe strongly in the power of their own convictions. This is at the heart of the type of faith that Werner and Smith (2001) described among individuals who believed that life would work out one way or another. It is a different quality than what we consider to be optimism, which is often described as hopefulness. Faith, for the purposes of resilience research, contains an element of trust and/or confidence, even if the source of that belief is hard to pin down or articulate.

Intuition and Exploration

Simply put, children are born curious. Teachers of young children know that young children are more capable than they are often assumed to be simply based on their sizes and/or ages. It is helpful to encourage children's developing understandings about the world, and to validate their instincts, gently correcting misperceptions and misinformation while supporting their inquisitive spirits. In one of my favorite books, fictional third-grader Justin Case shares his thoughts about how children are expected to behave and think, even when it doesn't make sense. His words capture typical childhood assumptions and resonate with grown-ups who also wonder about the sense behind some dominant opinions:

> Hurdles are this thing that's like running but watch out because whoops, in your way there are—I am not even joking—metal fence parts. Which obviously you should just go around. But no.

That is not true in camp. You have to somehow just jump right on over the fences. Like you are a cow and the fence is the moon.

As I was running toward the first hurdle, I was thinking about that nursery rhyme and why would people teach that to a kid? A cow can't jump over the moon. A cow can't jump over anything. There is so much kids need to learn in life, and they are new on the planet, so it is kind of mean to waste their time teaching them a cow jumps over the moon.

(Vail, 2012, p. 155)

Encouraging children to think independently means also teaching them to question answers and authorities. This skill is helpful when children feel rejected or are told they are wrong, yet they believe that they are fundamentally correct.

There are many stories of famous, successful people who attribute their successes to trusting their instincts, such as fashion designer Vera Wang, actor Sidney Poitier, and author J.K. Rowling. Teaching children to notice and honor their instincts will help them practice this skill so that they may draw upon their own inner wisdom in both ordinary and unusual circumstances. Noticing our instincts is one thing, and trusting our instincts is another. We have all heard family members or friends talk about how listening to those instincts has actually averted disaster in challenging moments. When stories about these kinds of moments are reported in various media channels, the reporters sometimes prompt us to think about what might have happened if someone had only listened to their instincts. But trusting one's inner voice is more than simply a skill to utilize in order to avoid tragedies. The activities included in this chapter encourage children to act in a way that may be counter to the norm, and to explore their instincts—indeed, their right—and choose the path of nonconformity if that is the path that, after weighing evidence and options, makes the most sense to them.

Social Competence and Resilience

Researchers who examine resilience have long recognized that some protective factors reside within the individual child, such as noticing one's instincts and choosing a path that leads to success. The competence that evolves over time as a result of these experiences extends beyond the individual into additional levels of protective factors. Different levels and the interactions between them have been examined in terms of the individual, the family, and the community (Fleming &

Ledogar, 2008; Luthar, Cicchetti, & Becker, 2000; Richards et al., 2016), recognizing that the different levels reflect unique qualities and characteristics. Fleming and Ledogar (2008), for example, added a category of cultural factors to their extensive list of protective social factors that contribute to resilience. These factors include spirituality, traditional activities, traditional languages, and traditional healing. As they explored cultural factors related to education, the authors noted that Native American educators have identified cultural resources that contribute to children's resilience—symbols and proverbs from a common language and culture, traditional child-rearing philosophies, religious leaders, counselors, and tribal elders.

How might such qualities translate into a classroom context? Project Competence, a longitudinal study led by Ann Masten, is anchored in questions such as this. Researchers involved with this project analyzed adversities and protective factors in the lives of 200 children and families from the Minneapolis Public Schools for over 20 years. In a recent interview, Masten noted that the research team wondered, "What are the everyday life experiences that people have and how is this related to how kids are doing at school?" "We were just interested in seeing how life experiences related to how you do later in life. We wanted to discover the resources and influences that make a difference. We also wanted to know: What helps children? What protects children?" (Steiner, 2014, pp. 2–3).

There are as many answers to those questions as there are new questions that emerge as a result of systematic inquiry. In the chapter that follows, the topic of motivation is explored. Motivation includes strategies that encourage children's self-regulation and skills that help young children achieve a positive balance that supports successful, healthy development into adolescence and adulthood, such as the ability to remain flexible in the face of complexity.

Turning Ideas Into Action

Questions to Your Questions

Goal: To teach children to search for deeper explanations in seemingly simple understandings. The aim is to do this in a way that arouses children's thinking, rather than stifles it, and bolsters self-esteem, rather than undermines it.

Materials needed: None, although paper/pencil or a dry-erase board can help record the flow of ideas

Action: Talk with children about Socrates, the Greek philosopher who lived over 2,500 years ago in Greece. For example, tell them, *"When people speak about Socrates today, it's often because of the way he taught people to think. He taught them to ask themselves questions about what they think. This is a special kind of thinking, and it is now named after him! It's called the Socratic method. Socrates was teaching people to question each other to get to the heart of their true beliefs and their own ways of knowing."* You can then choose one of the following prompts to begin a Socratic dialogue with the children in your class, or come up with one of your own:

> What makes someone strong?
> When should we let someone else win?
> How does a person prove she's smart?

The idea here is to begin with a question that seems rather simple and straightforward, and through the process of questioning and questioning again, the thoughts that you and the children generate will evolve until there is no longer any room for contradiction or questioning. Sometimes this takes a long time, and sometimes this moves more quickly. Here is an example of how this might flow:

Teacher: What makes someone strong?

Child: When they can do something no one else can do, they're strong.

Teacher: What if someone else can do the same thing? Are you not strong, even if you do the same thing as someone else?

Child: It's more special if not anyone could do it. If someone could get hurt or embarrassed that makes it different.

Teacher: So if there is risk involved, then that person is strong. Are there things that people do every day that don't involve risk, but are still strong?

Child: I guess giving something you like to someone you love is strong. And that can be a hard thing if the person giving something up really wants it.

Teacher: Does it matter whether a person does something strong so people can see, or can someone be strong in secret ways?

Child: Most of the time superheroes, like Wonder Woman or Spider-Man, are strong in public, because they're always saving people—but they're not really real. I think people can do things in secret that help people's lives, and if those things make a big difference, then that's strong.

Teacher: Does someone need to do something big to be strong, or can it be something small?

This back-and-forth continues until it feels to all like a natural resting point, or until the children are ready to move on to something else. The goal is to stimulate the children's thinking and to examine ideas from different angles than the one that's most obvious or agreed upon. You may be surprised at how children will continue to find new questions to extend the line of inquiry. If you find it difficult to get started, you can anchor a question in a common fable (e.g., the Tortoise and the Hare) or theme (e.g., if you can't say something nice, don't say anything at all), and see where the children guide the conversation.

Trust Your Gut

Goal: To help children recognize and honor their instincts and to validate their knowledge of the world

Materials needed: None, although paper and pen/pencil are helpful to record ideas

Action: Begin by inviting a small group of children to sit with you. This activity may also be used as a large group activity. Ask the children, *"Can you think of a time when you knew something was the right thing to do, and you followed your instinct? Sometimes people call this trusting your gut. Can you show me where your gut is?* (Point to your stomach.) *It's a long way from our brains! Sometimes we feel things and sometimes we think things."* Wait for them to respond with ideas, and if they have a hard time thinking of examples, try asking, *"Can you think of a time when you listened to your ideas or gut feelings? Do you sometimes question whether you are right or wrong? What happens?"*

As you listen to and discuss children's memories and ideas about trusting their "guts," you can discuss with them some strategies to help validate their instincts. These include:

- ◆ Quiet your mind—Explain that it's easier to pay attention to their instincts if they are able to find some quiet time to notice them. Try to find a few minutes each day to let children be someplace quiet, to notice their breathing (inhaling and exhaling), and to take a break from electronic tools or devices. This will naturally help them calm their minds and notice their thoughts and ideas.
- ◆ Notice your body and what it's telling you—Remind them that sometimes their bodies are able to tell them something

before they have a chance to think about it! They may remember times when their bodies have "told" them when they felt nervous, sad, angry, and other feelings. Explain that they can also focus on how their bodies respond to certain people in their environments. Explore this. *"Does seeing someone in particular cause you to feel something in your stomach, chest, or head? Noticing and listening to these sensations lets us realize much we know about ourselves and the world, even if we don't think about it at first."*

Children of various ages can participate in these discussions. While their ideas and abilities to articulate thoughts and feelings may be different, the benefits of sharing and connecting with others who share similar experiences make this a useful exercise.

The "Right" Move

Goal: To encourage children to think of alternative solutions or actions; to consider actions that move them closer to what they hope will happen, instead of acting because they're afraid of what might otherwise happen

Materials needed: A board game such as *Candyland, Chutes and Ladders*, or *Pay Day*—one that can provide useful visuals of a path with many steps

Action: If you have a board game available, you can show children how making one decision takes them down one path, and another decision, while somewhat risky because of potential conflict or loss, can actually move them closer to their goal. You may wish to play the board game with children, pausing to share examples of your own thinking and strategizing. For example, point out instances when you:

- ◆ Choose to redirect or delay progress in order to advance later
- ◆ Choose to take a modest risk to gain distance or reward
- ◆ Weigh a decision between two equally appealing/ unappealing decisions

Encourage children to ask questions if they don't understand your choices, and to argue for a different decision. The "right" move may look different to different people, and this is an opportunity to prove oneself correct when others would choose differently.

A Closer Look: Children's Behavior Through the "Resilience" Lens

Miranda smiled as she watched her son, Dylan, standing on third base—his six-foot-tall, lanky frame slouching in a "too cool for school" posture, hands in the back pockets of his baseball pants while he waited for the sign from the first-base coach. She felt the familiar boulder in her stomach. "Hello, anxiety! Nice to see you again!" she thought wryly. She wondered if she would ever simply be able to relax watching Dylan play baseball. She wondered if Dylan would ever simply be able to have fun playing baseball, and not judge himself more harshly than anyone else on the field, or on the planet! While she watched Dylan, memories played in her mind like film clips.

The preschool production of *The Very Hungry Caterpillar*—Families and friends were sitting in the child-sized chairs tucked together in the preschool classroom, listening eagerly to Alixe read the book aloud while children acted out the story as various characters (sun/moon, food items, caterpillar, butterfly). Dylan had been afraid to come out in his salami/cheese costume, and for five minutes that felt like an hour, the teachers had spoken softly and kindly with him, encouraging him to participate. Miranda had fought back tears, holding an internal conversation with herself about whether to step in or let the teachers handle the situation. She'd felt hot and cold at the same time, and she imagined that other parents were pitying her and Dylan because he was the only child visibly uncomfortable with the activity. She remembered the relief and elation she felt when Dylan timidly crept out on cue, looking cautiously at the room, and how the audience had clapped and cheered for him. In that moment she loved him more than she was certain her heart could contain, and she felt such gratitude for the support of the people in the room! She was so proud of Dylan.

Dorothy's office—Dylan was playing with the Incredible Hulk foam fists, which Dorothy often gave him to "smash" together to practice/play feeling strong. Dorothy suggested to Miranda that she and her husband Doug "build up" Dylan whenever they could, not with empty praise, but by pointing out his efforts and strengths. It was Dorothy who recommended the 80:20 rule—let children win board games 80% of the time, even if you know you could win the game. This was her advice in response to parents wondering whether or not they should let their children win, or whether they should play games as they typically would, though that meant that the grown-ups would have a distinct advantage. "Build him up when you can," Dorothy had said. "He's already hard on himself."

Sitting in the car after pickup one day in fifth grade—"I just think of school like prison," Dylan had said. "I just deal with it." Miranda felt like she'd been punched in the stomach. Subsequent talks with Mr. O'Shea, the guidance counselor, had revealed that the fifth-grade boys were a particularly difficult bunch in terms of behavior. They'd earned a reputation across the district, and he felt that Dylan was struggling to feel anchored in a sea of alpha boys and with a young classroom teacher that was substituting for the teacher of record, out for months on an extended medical leave. Mr. O'Shea acknowledged that it could be challenging for a sensitive boy like Dylan, and Miranda had said that if Dylan were a superhero, his superpower would be empathy. He was truly gifted in that regard.

Dylan leaning over the toilet in the bathroom off the kitchen—For the first month of ninth grade, Dylan threw up every morning—except weekends! It was clear that going to school was causing him the upset, but different strategies and attempts to identify clear causes of concern had resulted in limited success. Dylan did not fear being bullied, he did not struggle with classwork, and he had a group of friends. Once he got to school, he was fine, but it was the morning vomiting ritual that caused Miranda stress and concern, and she and Doug felt helpless because they couldn't "fix" the problem. Miranda sought the help of a psychologist, Ben, who Dylan began meeting with once a week. Over time, the morning ritual had subsided, and the throwing up became associated strictly with baseball—games, clinics, and practices, it didn't matter. Once Dylan got onto the field, however, he was fine.

Miranda watched Dylan run to and cross home plate, then trot to the dugout to sit with the rest of his teammates. She grinned, thinking that people are all wired so differently. She knew she couldn't protect Dylan from pain and disappointment. She just wished he didn't feel things as deeply or acutely as he did. No—she corrected herself. She wished he could have those feelings *and* then tuck them away without judging himself so harshly.

She reminded herself that no matter what the challenge was, Dylan *always* met that challenge. He never hid from it or crawled under the covers and refused to come out.

"Man, growing up is hard," she thought. "And that's just the parenting part!" she thought in the next second, chuckling a bit—out loud, she realized. She pretended to cough and continued watching the game.

Resources

826 National
https://826national.org

One of this organization's core values is that "everyone is respected, included, and heard." 826 National teaches children the transformative powers of writing. Staff and community volunteers create and learn with children in seven cities across the U.S., encouraging them to develop their own creative self-expression and to recognize their own power and potential.

Every Child Matters
http://everychildmatters.org

This organization is anchored in the belief that when children's issues become a priority, then families, communities, and the overall economy all benefit. Focusing on topics such as poverty, discrimination, and other barriers to success, this organization provides resources to help all children succeed.

Quiet Revolution
www.quietrev.com

Responding to the misperception that extroverts are successful and introverts are somehow deficient, Susan Cain's book *Quiet* inspired this organization, whose mission includes celebrating individual differences as strengths. With supports such as "Parenting and Kids" and the "Quiet Schools Network," this organization promotes new understandings and opportunities for children to honor and develop their unique selves.

References

Boyce, W.T., & Ellis, B.J. (2005). Biological sensitivity to context, Vol. 1: An evolutionary-developmental theory of the origins and functions of stress reactivity. *Developmental Psychology, 17*(2), 271–301.

De Bono, E. (1993). *Teach your child how to think*. London, England: Penguin Books.

Fleming, J., & Ledogar, R.J. (2008). Resilience, an evolving concept: A review of literature relevant to aboriginal research. *Pimatisiwin, 6*(2), 7–23.

Freire, P. (2000). *Pedagogy of the oppressed: 30th anniversary edition*. New York, NY: Bloomsbury Academic.

Gladwell, M. (2005). *Blink: The power of thinking without thinking*. New York: Back Bay Books.

Greenfield, K. (2011). *The myth of choice: Personal responsibility in a world of limits*. New Haven: Yale University Press.

Greitens, E. (2015). *Resilience: Hard-won wisdom for living a better life*. Boston, MA: Houghton Mifflin Harcourt Publishing Company.

Herbert, W. (2011). On the trail of the orchid child: One genetic variant leads to the best and worst outcomes in kids. *Scientific American*. Retrieved from https://www.scientificamerican.com/article/on-the-trail-of-the-orchid-child/

Krovetz, M.L. (2008). *Fostering resilience: Expecting all students to use their minds and hearts well*. Thousand Oaks, CA: Corwin Press.

Luthar, S.S., Cicchetti, D., & Becker, B. (2000). The construct of resilience: A critical evaluation and guidelines for future work. *Child Development, 71*(3), 543–562.

Marcus, G. (2008). Total recall. *The New York Times Magazine*. Retrieved from https://www.nytimes.com/2008/04/13/magazine/13wwln-essay-t.html

Maslow, A. (1954). *Motivation and personality*. New York: Harper.

Masten, A. (2014, January/February). Global perspectives on resilience in children and youth. *Child Development, 85*(1), 6–20.

Masten, A. (2015, June). *Resilience in human development: Interdependent adaptive systems in theory and action*. Presentation at Pathways to Resilience III, at the University of Minnesota, Minneapolis, MN. Retrieved from www.resilienceresearch.org/files/PTR/AnnMasten-PTRKeynote.pdf

Palacio, R.J. (2012). *Wonder*. New York, NY: Alfred A. Knopf.

Richards, M., Romero, E., Deane, K., Carey, D., Zakaryan, A., Quimby, D., . . . Patel, N. (2016, March). Civic engagement curriculum: A strengths-based intervention serving African American youth in a context of toxic stress. *Journal of Child & Adolescent Trauma, 9*(1), 81–93.

Shakur, T. (1999). *The rose that grew from concrete.* New York, NY: MTV Books and Pocket Books.

Steiner, A. (2014, September 17). Ann Masten: Children's natural resilience is nurtured through "ordinary magic". *MinnPost.* Retrieved from www.minnpost.com/mental-health-addiction/ 2014/09/ann-masten-children-s-natural-resilience-nurtured-through-ordinary-m

Vail, R. (2012). *Justin Case: Shells, smells, and the horrible flip-flops of doom.* New York, NY: Feiwel and Friends.

Werner, E.E. (1995). Resilience in development. *Current Directions in Psychological Science, 4*(3), 81–85.

Werner, E.E., & Smith, R.S. (2001). *Journeys from childhood to midlife: Risk, resilience, & recovery.* Ithaca, NY: Cornell University Press.

4

Constructing an Understanding of Motivation

In the beautifully written and illustrated children's book *Crow Boy* (Yashima, 1976), the protagonist, Chibi, is considered weak and odd by his peers and elders. One teacher believes in and supports him, and eventually Chibi demonstrates his wisdom and skills, inspiring awe and respect from those who had long misunderstood him. Elements of this story echo the concepts of grit and resilience presented in the previous chapters, and for the purposes of this chapter it serves as an effective example for the role of motivation in future development. In the broadest optimistic sense,

> [e]ffectively weaving social, emotional, and academic compo-
> nents into the fabric of a school helps students remain moti-
> vated to develop skills to navigate and succeed within their
> learning communities and to serve as responsible, contributing
> members of society.
>
> (ASPEN Institute, 2017, p. 3)

Those critical of the pressures that children experience inside and out of the classroom underscore key positions discussed in previous chapters, such as the arguments that stress and hardship do *not* better prepare children to face life's difficulties, and that encouraging people to pressure themselves "may buy success at school or work at the cost of a substantially lower quality of life" (Kohn, 2017, par. 7).

Assuming that quality of life and joy in learning are always at the core of teaching objectives, it is important to acknowledge that there are indeed times when emotions—such as fear—can serve a constructive purpose, motivating students to reach a goal. Consider the fight-or-flight response described in Chapter 2, where fear is directly linked to survival. Researchers suggest that when we worry about a situation or potential risk, we pay more attention to it and take action as needed. "Fear keeps us alive and thriving. It's no exaggeration to say that our species owes its very existence to fear" (Gardner, 2008, p. 6). Furthermore, "fear is a crucial link in the cognitive chain; behind the scenes, it helps nudge us in the right direction" (Clark, 2011, p. 137). It is important to recognize, however, when fear becomes a mechanism to avoid failure, rather than a motivational force to achieve success. When this happens, the motivation is less likely to contribute constructively to a child's development in the long term (Kohn, 2017).

In the extensive media coverage of the 2018 Winter Olympics (a.k.a. the XXIII Olympic Winter Games) held in PyeongChang, stories of athletes' personal motivation were presented before, during, and after specific events. The stories introduced athletes to the viewing public, who served as examples of individuals whose grit, resilience, and *motivation* contributed to their Olympic dreams becoming a reality. Figure 4.1 is one of many social media items designed to

Figure 4.1 Elmotivation Tweet

inspire followers. In this example, children are the target audience, though there is a touch of irony in terms of who actually pays for and facilitates a child's Olympic journey, as well as who owns the device to receive and actually read the tweet. These fine, discrete elements will be discussed later in this chapter, in terms of intrinsic and extrinsic motivation.

In the section that follows, we will examine definitions and theories related to motivation, and the specific role of motivation in the classroom context.

Definitions and Theories

When we understand child development and how children think, we know that their cognitive development proceeds rapidly during early childhood. They move from the more concrete to the more abstract thinking, and they use repetition and play to help understand concepts through their own lenses. These lenses are, at least generally, limited to their own lived experiences—both "real-life" experiences and "virtual" experiences that are brought about through television and computer programming—and sometimes the boundaries are blurred.

Mental Maps

In the field of intellectual development, psychologist Edward Tolman (1948) used the term "cognitive maps" to describe a person's mental representations of the environment. He coined the term as the result of research in which he studied rats and how they worked their way through mazes to attain their rewards. Tolman argued that people, like the laboratory animals, use mental representations to recall important information and to find their way in a literal sense. Extending this concept to a metaphorical sense, as children grow over time, they construct and use these cognitive maps to "find their way" in academic and social situations as well. Different situations provide children with many opportunities to create these mental maps, including "objects, pathways, and rewards" (Hallinan, 2009, p. 175).

Asking children to draw their own maps of a given place or situation provides teachers and caregivers with insight into what elements children tune into, and what they consider to be important information, as compared with information that may be discarded. These choices inform adults about what is more or less important at any given moment in time, and maps can be compared over time to notice changes in children's perspectives and values.

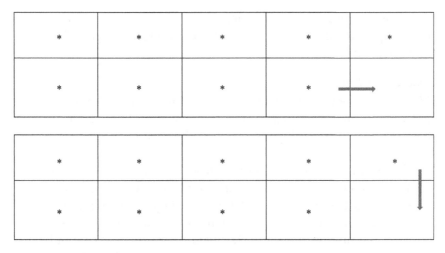

Figure 4.2 10-frame Example

Author Joseph Hallinan argues that "much of life, arguably, boils down to finding the shortcut to the cheese. . . . So how do we go about solving the 1,001 problems we face each day?" (Hallinan, 2009, p. 175). He further notes that people generally do not like to follow directions or read instructions—they prefer to do something different, "and much of what we do read we either ignore or don't understand" (p. 176).

Can you think of classroom examples when a concept is taught a certain way and children—and more often, adults—tend to stick to this one way of learning and explaining something? As a simple example, an ordinary 10-frame math lesson in a kindergarten classroom could feature the question, "Is 9 closer to 5 or to 10?" A sample 10-frame could look like the top example in Figure 4.2.

Most children in the United States would look at the image and respond that 9 is closer to 10 because of the way that American children learn to read English—horizontally, left to right, top to bottom of a page. But some children might think about this differently, and notice that 9 is just as close to 5 as it is to 10, as illustrated in the bottom example. Each square is one square away from the other—in fact, the 5 and 9 squares share separate sides of the 10 square. This type of functional flexibility runs counter to the functional "fixity" that Hallinan describes.

Yet over time, and as they learn more information that they can connect to previously learned information, children tend to solve problems using one approach that works and that has proven effective over time. This tendency often prevails when children are faced with simple problems because they come to learn that efficiency and accuracy are more important than creativity, and are therefore motivated by certainty over risk.

Head Versus Gut

Educators are not always comfortable with the idea that much of what motivates human thinking is unconscious, evolutionary hardwiring that is as simple as finding a shortcut to the cheese, or other reward:

> "I am not willing to assume," wrote David Brooks, the *New York Times* columnist, "that our brains are like computers. . . . Isn't it just as possible that the backstage part of the brain [meaning unconscious thought] might be more like a personality, some unique and nontechnological essence that cannot be adequately generalized about by scientists in white coats with clipboards?" What Brooks is saying here is what many of us vaguely sense: that the brain is a big, complex, physical organ at the center of which is some indefinable thing or entity that makes decisions and issues commands for reasons scientists in white coats will never be able to fathom.
>
> (Gardner, 2008, p. 21)

Author Daniel Gardner describes two systems—System One ("gut") and System Two ("head")—which work semi-independently of each other, with continuous, complicated interactions between them. For example, "[i]t's possible that knowledge learned and used consciously by Head can sink into the unconscious mind, to be used by Gut" (p. 27). Whereas System One—"gut"—is the hardwired, intuitive system that informs our thinking, System Two—"head"—is slower, incorporating reason.

He notes how people use common expressions such as "I have a gut feeling," when we know something to be true but cannot quite articulate why it is so, or "use your head," when we want someone to slow down and think before acting. "Gut decides, head reviews: This process is how most of our thoughts and decisions are made" (p. 29). It is important to note, however, a false separation of the two domains— knowledge in the head versus feelings in the gut or heart. Gardner notes that "in reality the brain alone generates all thoughts and feelings" (Gardner, 2008, p. 26), and in Chapter 7 we will explore the relationship between thinking and feeling. It is interesting to consider, however, the role of sensory input and the interplay between thinking and feeling, and how this impacts motivation and development.

Carol Dweck

The work of psychologist and author Carol Dweck has, over the past 30 years, greatly influenced teaching and learning at every level of schooling, from classroom to central office, student to superintendent. The term "growth mindset" (Dweck, 1988) has become common parlance in educational settings, and part of the appeal is the scientific research that serves as a strong foundation for developing classroom and school practices.

Dweck and her associates describe patterns that they categorize into "helpless" and "mastery-oriented" learning approaches and behaviors. They argue that these patterns explain psychological processes that children display when they are presented with problem-solving challenges. Over time, in numerous discrete studies, researchers noticed that children possess specific dispositions and leanings—implicit theories that incline them toward particular goals—and that these goals form the patterns over time (Dweck & Leggett, 1988).

In short, helpless children viewed their difficulties as failure, as indicative of low ability, and as insurmountable. They appeared to view further effort as futile and, perhaps, as their defensive maneuvers suggest, as further documentation of their inadequate ability.

> In striking contrast, the mastery-oriented children, when confronted with the difficult problems, did not begin to offer attributions for their failure. Indeed, they did not appear to think they were failing. Rather than viewing unsolved problems as failures that reflected on their ability, they appeared to view the unsolved problems as challenges to be mastered through effort.
>
> (Dweck & Leggett, 1988, p. 258)

From these findings emerged vocabulary that describes children's mindsets—their beliefs about their abilities to learn something and demonstrate that learning effectively.

Dweck describes a child who believes that her efforts will always lead to less or unsuccessful outcomes as possessing a *fixed mindset*. The child believes that she either knows something or doesn't, or is good at something or isn't. In a classroom setting, this mindset contributes to an urgent need to prove oneself over and over (Dweck, 2016). In her writing and speaking engagements, Dweck often cites her own sixth-grade classroom experience—the teacher seated the students in IQ order, and "only the highest-IQ students could be trusted to carry the flag, clap the erasers, or take a note to the principal" (Dweck, 2016, p. 6). This instilled in students a tremendous fear of losing a prized seat in a particular row, as well as the motivation to keep that seat at all costs.

In contrast, a *growth mindset* is based on a child's belief that her fundamental qualities and skills can be developed and supported through effort. Effort can include strategies that a child thinks of on her own, as well as those learned by seeking or accepting help from others. In a classroom setting, this mindset is evident when a child understands lack of success as something that can change with more practice or exposure to the material in new and different ways. The most important element of this mindset and how it translates into a classroom can be boiled down to the simple assertion that "everyone can change and grow through application and experience" (Dweck, 2016, p. 7).

What does this mean for classrooms and schools? In some cases it requires a radical culture shift in which educators recognize that children are not fixed entities, and that human qualities are not set in stone. No one is "smart" in an all-encompassing way, and taking risks and making mistakes reflect strength and curiosity as much as they reflect areas to be developed. In this way, students learn to accept successes and failures as part of a broader, evolving learning process. It also means that some measures, such as standardized tests, reflect students' abilities at one moment in time but they do not accurately capture or reflect *potential*. Just as scientific research has been touting the idea that people's brains have greater capacity for lifelong learning (a.k.a. neuroplasticity), education policy and practice is beginning to champion a similar stance, in which children are viewed as learners with the power to determine for themselves how much effort they will apply, and therefore how successful they might be in a given task or domain. "[S]tudents often haven't learned that working hard involves thinking hard, which involves reflecting on and changing our strategies so we become more and more effective learners over time, and we need to guide them to come to understand this" (Briceño, 2015).

If young children learn that their own personal qualities and abilities can change over time with effort and motivation, then over the course of their lifetimes they are more likely to confront challenges, persist in the face of obstacles, and develop more effective learning strategies (Briceño, 2015). Taking the long view, Dweck posits that "[t]he *view you adopt for yourself* profoundly affects the way you lead your life. It can determine whether you become the person you want to be and whether you accomplish the things you value" (Dweck, 2016, p. 6).

Objectivity Versus Subjectivity

It is hard sometimes to separate what we believe to be true and what we believe *should be* true. As we develop from children into adults, we have the benefit of lived experiences against which we can compare present moments to maintain some healthy perspective. Young children, however, absolutely live *in* the current moment. Teachers of young children can support children's motivation by providing them with opportunities to gain some distance and perspective in order to persist toward a desired goal. The activities at the end of this chapter, for example, are designed to promote practice with these and related skills that are described in the sections that follow.

Calibration

In a general sense, elements that contribute to the development of motivation include:

◆ Autonomy—our desire to be self-directed
◆ Mastery—our urge to get better at what we do
◆ Purpose—our yearning to be part of something larger than ourselves

(Pink, 2009, p. 10)

Researchers in the field of social science call the ability to realize one's own limitations *calibration*. This term refers to a person's perception of her abilities and her actual abilities or limitations. Calibration measures the gap between perception and reality. A person with an accurate sense of her own abilities is said to be well calibrated, while a person who has an inflated sense of her own abilities is said to be poorly calibrated (Hallinan, 2009).

To illustrate this term, Hallinan presents meteorologists as a group that, in his opinion, are well-calibrated professionals:

[S]imply telling farmers there was a "chance" of rain wasn't good enough; they had too much at risk. They needed to know if that chance was a 50 percent change, a 75 percent chance, or a 100 percent chance.

(Hallinan, 2009, p. 156)

Once forecasters started including probabilities with their forecasts, they were able to quantify their predictions. "As a result, weather forecasters have established a long track record of predictions [and] have a record of the actual results" (p. 157).

Calculation

Another consideration of how people assess their resources and make decisions is featured in the work of psychologists Amos Tversky and Daniel Kahneman (1974). Though conducted decades ago, their research feels quite relevant today. Their research partnership grew in response to their curiosity and intuition about human judgment, as well as their discomfort with the perceived lack of self-reflection and self-awareness that they witnessed in male authority figures. For decades,

> the dominant model . . . was that of *Homo economicus*. "Economic man" is supremely rational. He examines evidence. He calculates what would best advance his interests as he understands them, and he acts accordingly.
>
> (Gardner, 2008, p. 39)

Kahneman and Tversky showed that "in certain circumstances, people *always* make mistakes" (Gardner, 2008, p. 40). At the time their work gained widespread attention in a new field—decision analysis—these researchers were hopeful that they could convince leaders to examine their own decision-making systems and generate quantitative measurements that helped them evaluate decisions in terms of the process, rather than the outcome. When their work was ready to be shared broadly with the public, they chose to publish their work in *Science* because they desired a wide reach and believed that their work held appeal for scientists *and* non-scientists.

Gardner (2008) includes the work of Kahneman and Tversky as he describes what he calls "The Rule of Typical Things":

> When there's something "typical" involved, our intuition is triggered. It just feels right. And as always with intuitive feelings, we tend to go with them even when doing so flies in the face of logic and evidence. . . . Another problem is that the Rule of Typical Things is only as good as our knowledge of what is "typical."
>
> (p. 43)

So it seems that all human experience may be complicated by what a person feels and what she thinks. As much as we would like to think that we control our thinking and our decision-making, researchers continue to show that there is no clear-cut way to explain why we feel, think, or act. Sometimes the root influences on a child's motivation can be traced to the basic desire to please someone she loves, respects, or even fears.

In a humorous recollection of how he became motivated to eat his vegetables, Newberg recalls:

> One day [my mother] tried a different approach: guilt. She told me that the peas on the plate would be lonely if I left them there because they wouldn't be with their friends. Their friends, of course, were the peas I had already reluctantly eaten. Suddenly, I saw my plate in an entirely different light. Peas, I realized, had feelings—and friends!
>
> (Newberg & Waldman, 2006, p. 103)

Sometimes children are motivated simply because they care about what others think, or how they perform (nature), yet educators also must examine the influence of the environment (nurture) on children's motivation.

Intrinsic Versus Extrinsic Motivation

Schools, like societies, have systems that children come to know and internalize—rules, customs, instructions, protocols, and understandings about how the world works. There is interplay between internal and external forces as a child attempts to make sense of the world or, in this case, a classroom setting. While the motivation that a child brings into a classroom may be influenced by intrinsic and/or extrinsic forces, it is interesting to consider times when a perceived lack of motivation might actually be advantageous.

The Role of Caution

Author Sarah Elizabeth Adler (2018) notes the role of caution, and even pessimism, in connection with children's performance. In a recent "study of studies" featured in *The Atlantic*, she notes that there are some instances when "pessimists fare better than those with a sunnier disposition" (p. 25). Adler presents the conclusions of over a dozen studies, which include findings like:

- ◆ Feeling down can make us behave more fairly
- ◆ Bad moods are linked to a more effective communication style
- ◆ Optimism can result in disappointment

This latter point, underscoring a "glass is half-empty" mindset, was described years ago as a "defensive pessimism" (Norem & Cantor, 1986), which is essentially very similar to preparing for the worst. There may be some significant evolutionary wisdom to this approach.

Tens of thousands of years ago, human behavior could be connected to one overarching goal—survival. Researchers agree that it was the main biological drive that guided most of humans' behaviors. Over time, "[a]s humans formed more complex societies, bumping up against strangers and needing to cooperate in order to get things done, an operating system based purely on biological drive was inadequate" (Pink, 2009, pp. 17–18). The connection to motivation is sometimes as simple as the desire "to seek reward and avoid punishment more broadly" (Pink, 2009, p. 18). Teachers attempt to harness this knowledge in their classrooms, knowing that a successful way to improve performance, increase productivity, and encourage excellence is to reward the good and punish the bad (p. 19).

Sometimes, however, this idea can have the opposite effect. Researchers Lepper, Greene, and Nisbett (1973) conducted a study focused on the premise that "a person's intrinsic interest in an activity may be decreased by inducing him to engage in that activity as an explicit means to some extrinsic goal" (p. 129). Such situations, they suggest, occur frequently in traditional classrooms where systems of extrinsic rewards—whether grades, gold stars, or the awarding of special privileges—are applied as a matter of course to an entire class of children (pp. 135–136).

This may at first seem confusing, because humans grow up setting goals and striving to achieve them:

> From our earliest days, teachers, coaches, and parents advise us to set goals and to work mightily to achieve them—and with good reason. Goals work. The academic literature shows that . . . goals can get us to try harder, work longer, and achieve more.
> (Pink, 2009, p. 50)

The distinction lies in terms of who sets the goals. Goals that people set for themselves and that are devoted to attaining mastery are usually healthy, but goals imposed by others, such as standardized test scores, can sometimes have negative side effects. On the one hand, goals help children narrow their focus. They can therefore be effective as they encourage children to concentrate on a specific task. On the other hand, a narrowed focus can hinder the type of thinking necessary to come up with a creative solution. Pink (2009) argues that "when an extrinsic goal is paramount—particularly a short-term, measurable one whose achievement delivers a big payoff—its presence can restrict our view of the broader dimensions of our behavior" (p. 50).

Teachers who recall even the most basic psychological principles of behaviorism understand the combination of reward and punishment that can be used to increase a desired behavior, and the metaphor of "carrot and stick." Pink (2009) summarizes the dangers associated with methods or incentives used to motivate children toward desired results as follows:

1. They can extinguish intrinsic motivation.
2. They can diminish performance.
3. They can crush creativity.
4. They can crowd out good behavior.
5. They can encourage cheating, shortcuts, and unethical behavior.
6. They can become addictive.
7. They can foster short-term thinking.

(p. 59)

Author and educator Vanessa Rodriguez (2014) refocuses the lens on the teacher—on teaching and learning on a cognitive level—when she asks,

Is it a successful learning experience if an A on a paper comes only after a month of sleepless nights, or if a 100 on a test is the grand prize for puking? My suspicion is that most teachers— indeed, most people—would think not. More to the point, what do grades tell us absent any awareness of the actual experience of learning, of the process that a learner undergoes to earn those marks?

(p. 47)

Indeed, research has shown that the most satisfying, rewarding experiences in children's lives are those when they set their own goals, and when the activity itself is its own reward.

The Role of Flow

Perhaps the most well-known description of moments such as this is what psychologist Mihaly Csikszentmihalyi (2008) describes as "flow." He arrived at this term over the course of research in which he noted that, in the midst of play, many people experienced these optimal moments.

Regardless of the activity, individuals in "flow" experienced a sense of discovery, as well as a feeling of being swept away into a new reality that drove the person toward higher levels of creativity and, ultimately, performance. As a result, the individual self was transformed because the activity inspired growth through engagement.

What brings about flow varies from person to person and depends in part on the relationship between what a person can do and must do. For example, a professional athlete—playing a game that people typically associate with fun—might actually be "playing" without any of the elements of flow being present. The person could be going through the motions, be concerned about impressing a scout, or be feeling self-conscious, rather than focusing on and enjoying the game. Interestingly, Csikszentmihalyi (2008) notes that

> the opposite is even more likely—that a person will deeply enjoy activities that were intended for other purposes. To many people activities like working or raising children provide more flow than playing a game or painting a picture, because these individuals have learned to perceive opportunities in such mundane tasks that others do not see.

(p. 76)

Figure 4.3 Hopscotch Fun

For teachers of young children, the challenge lends itself to designing engaging classroom activities that set the stage for children to experience flow—experiences that are not too easy, nor too difficult. These activities can inspire a child to reach beyond her current abilities, in ways that stretch her thinking and increase her skill sets, making the effort a reward in itself. When children are engaged in such an all-encompassing manner—with clear, attainable goals well suited to their interests and abilities—they are motivated to learn without external rewards.

The Role of Rewards

Author Alfie Kohn notes that as children progress through elementary school, their motivation and approach to learning becomes increasingly extrinsic (Kohn, 1999). He cautions that when "do this and you'll get that" is the rule rather than the exception in children's classroom experiences, they come to believe that their efforts are wasted unless there are extrinsic rewards (Kohn, 1999).

In his book *Punished by Rewards*, Kohn (1999) examines the influence that rewards have on children's potential for learning and for enjoying the learning process. He identifies some key facts, including the fact that young children do not need to be rewarded in order to learn: "[T]he fact that children are not equally receptive to what the teacher is doing at any given moment should not distract us from recognizing that the desire to learn itself is natural" (p. 144). Furthermore, Kohn states that throughout human development, "rewards are less effective than intrinsic motivation for promoting effective learning," and "children are more likely to be optimal learners if they are interested in what they are learning" (p. 144). Kohn is critical of the current educational climate that holds children accountable for their achievement when they do not set the goals for their own learning. "When rewards don't succeed at enhancing students' interest and achievement, we offer—new rewards. . . . When this too proves ineffective, we put the blame on the students themselves, deciding that they must lack ability or are just too lazy to make an effort" (p. 143). This type of feedback not only detracts from joy in learning for learning's sake and experiencing flow, but also deters children from taking risks that could lead to inspiring discoveries.

The Role of Feedback

In the most simplistic sense, feedback provides children with information about what action has been taken and the results that have followed. In the realm of science, feedback lets a person know whether something has been done correctly. Experts note that feedback "is a powerful way to shape human behavior. It's why slot machines pay out immediately. Casinos want you to keep doing what you're doing" (Hallinan, 2009, p. 158).

For children, positive feedback may inspire them to reach new heights and take some careful risks to stretch their thinking. But feedback in the form of pressure can also motivate children "to jump higher or memorize more facts for awhile. But is the point to avoid failure or to achieve success? Those are two very different things" (Kohn, 2017, par. 6). There is a fine balance to strike between praising effort or ability and increasing the pressure that a child feels to please or to perform for the sake of achieving a goal set by others. For teachers of young children, when the primary goals include engaging curriculum, relationships among children and adults, and a classroom environment that reflects caring and respect, motivation will be authentic and visible.

As we continue to think about the role of early childhood educators in nurturing children's qualities that will help them succeed in the broadest sense, the activities and resources below are provided to support and motivate children along their developmental journey. In the two chapters that follow, we focus on specific factors that can create difficulties for children and place them at risk. The concepts of grit, resilience, and motivation will be examined in relation to these topics and to classroom applications that promote empowerment.

Turning Ideas Into Action

What Happens on Opposite Day?
Goal: To encourage children to consider alternatives to generally accepted stories or values

Materials needed: None are required, but favorite children's books can provide concrete images and language to draw upon, as needed

Action: Here are some suggested conversation starters to choose from:

- ◆ Familiar endings to well-known stories
    - *What if T'Challa did not protect the nation of Wakanda?*
    - *What if Snow White didn't marry Prince Charming?*
    - *What if Harry Potter didn't defeat Voldemort?*
    - *What if the Hulk emerged when Bruce Banner got extremely happy instead of angry, and his strength increased with the level of happiness?*

◆ Familiar phenomena
- *What if rain fell up, not down?*
- *What if elephants were tiny and mice were huge?*
- *What if we ate cake and ice cream for dinner and carrots and broccoli for dessert?*

Children will enjoy this activity as written, and can extend their thinking to consider alternate outcomes for real-life, current events. For example, *What if cars and trucks used potatoes instead of gasoline as fuel?* or *What if teachers earned more money than football players?*

Attitude Forecast

Goal: To develop awareness of feelings in the moment and notice that negative feelings are temporary; to notice how a positive outlook can boost one's mood and help us persist toward a goal

Materials needed: Images of weather scenes (clouds, sunshine, rain, wind), either drawn, printed out from the Internet, or cut from magazines

Action: Children are often familiar with the process of looking out the window, noticing the weather, and declaring whether the forecast looks to be sunny, rainy, or other. This same process can be used to notice their own mood outlooks. Talk with the children about how sometimes when we feel sunny or positive, we also feel like we can accomplish something, and we don't think about giving up. Other times, we might feel sad, or soggy/rainy, and this can sometimes make us feel like we can't accomplish something. We therefore focus on the negative aspects of a situation.

Attitude Forecast

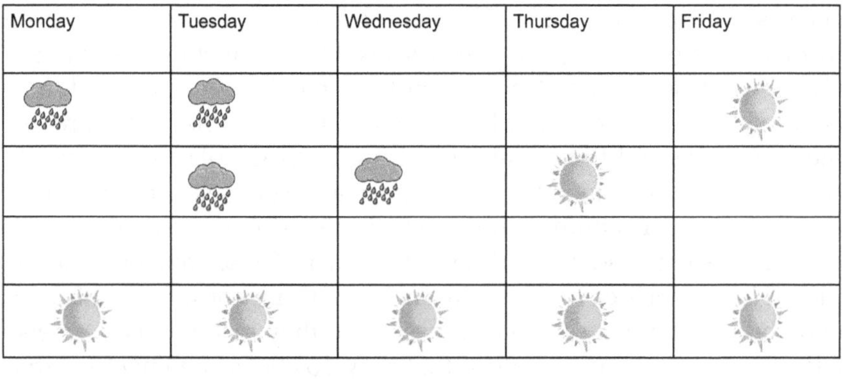

Monday	Tuesday	Wednesday	Thursday	Friday
🌧	🌧			☀
	🌧	🌧	☀	
☀	☀	☀	☀	☀

Figure 4.4 Attitude Forecast Chart

Role-play with students how you might check in with your own self or body to notice how you are feeling. You may wish to model this check-in with students about their own "weather" report several times a day, and keep a "weather" chart to display your own and the children's attitudes over time. Over the course of a few days, you'll likely notice patterns. For example, you might notice that after recess the children report feeling sunny more often, or on days when they have several specialists back-to-back, there are more reports of cloudy or rainy "weather." This activity helps children connect their own feelings to external forces, and also empowers them to change what they can in that moment to bring about a change in the "weather"—their attitudes.

Can-Do Cards for Kids

Goal: To provide external motivation for children when their own motivation is running low

Materials needed: Pre-written cards in labeled envelopes

Action: This is an activity that you can introduce by modeling for the children in your class, and very quickly they will be able to write motivational cards for each other and for others that they know and care about.

Begin by preparing envelopes that feature statements like the following (or images that reflect these sentiments) on them:

"Open when you feel frustrated"
"Open when your energy is low"
"Open when you feel scared"
"Open when you want to give up"
"Open when you miss someone you love"

Inside the envelopes, you can choose to write inspirational comments such as "I believe in you!" or "You are so loved!" You may also choose to place images of inspiring scenes inside the envelopes, such as a stunning sunset, or athletes (e.g., professional, Paralympics, children) crossing a finish line or reaching a goal. Small objects that represent meaning to the children are also inspiring, such as a photo of a favorite school community member (e.g., specialist, counselor, food service employee) giving a thumbs-up, or a soft, silky ribbon or small, smooth stone that is cool and comforting to the touch. These envelopes can be placed in a quiet area in the room, such as a peace corner or book area, and children can visit the envelopes when they feel the need, or else friends and others may suggest that they go choose an envelope that can be selected and read to them, if needed.

Extension: As children tend to know each other so well, they may choose to create "mail" for each other when they notice that their peers could use some extra support. Having mailboxes for children in the classroom is one place that these envelopes may be delivered throughout the day, and cubbies work well as alternatives. Raising awareness about their own and others' feelings will be discussed in greater detail in Chapters 7 and 8.

A Closer Look: Children's Behavior Through the Motivation Lens

"I am going to write a book one day, called *100 Ways My Father Tortured Me*," Liling said, laughing. Kevin looked at her, raising his eyebrows and smiling, with an expression on his face that suggested he was thinking, "Really?"

"I'm serious!" she said, continuing to smile. "My father was so mean. Chinese parents put so much pressure on their children— it's just the way it is. Like, if you don't do well on this math test, you should feel bad, because this other person did really well on the math test!"

Liling and Kevin were classmates in a class titled Teaching, Learning, and Social Responsibility, and the topic of equity and access to resources had prompted much animated discussion between them, carrying them out of the classroom and over to the campus café to continue their discussion.

"But you're not really afraid your dad will *hurt* you?" Kevin asked, his eyes wide.

"Oh yes! He would fight me!" Liling replied, laughing. "When he gets mad my mom always quickly leaves the room! He's not that way with my little sister, though—we're very different. One time, in first grade, he talked to me after school. He told me that I hadn't done well on the math test but the neighbor—a person my age—had done very well. He told me that I had to stand in the corner of the walls and think about how I did and what I could do to do better the next time." She took a sip of her coffee, then swallowed and laughed, exclaiming, "He must have forgotten about me! I think I was there for like three hours. I fell asleep! Standing up against the wall, I fell asleep!" Kevin laughed and shook his head, smiling.

"One time," Liling said, "there was this essay competition for students in second grade. I told my dad I didn't want to do the competition. He said ok."

"And then?" Kevin asked, pointing to a cookie Liling had bought.

"And then my father said to me, 'You know, you don't have to do the essay, but maybe you should practice writing an outline. Go write an outline of what you would write if you *were going to* do the essay.' So I went off and wrote and outline and showed my father. He gave me some feedback and I really liked that he was talking with me about it."

"The next day, my father said, 'You know, you already did the outline. You should write a draft of the essay—just a draft—as if you *were going to* write the essay for the competition.' So I went off to my room and wrote a few pages and then showed my father. He liked it and gave me more feedback about what I could change or do better. So the next day I wrote another draft. After a few days, I had written the essay! Of course I turned it in. My father got me to do it and I didn't even know I was doing it! But it was good for me." She smiled, passing Kevin a piece of cookie.

"Wow—your dad is sneaky!" Kevin said. "That must have been kind of hard for you growing up. Did you worry that he might not love you or something if you didn't do well?"

"My father never talks about loving me! That's not the way he is. He works very hard and it is very important to him and to my mother that we give something back to the world. In our city there is a place—like a recycling place—where my father and mother will take my sister and me to wash the bottles or other things. They do it, too! They don't even use gloves, because after a while the smell is so bad." She paused, then continued dramatically, slapping her hand flat on the tabletop. "The smell is so bad, but after a while you don't mind it anymore and so you don't worry about wearing gloves. My parents want my sister and me to know that we need to work hard, but they do it, too, so we can't really complain about the treatment!"

"Whoa—that's pretty cool, and smelly!" Kevin said. "I don't think my parents would ever do something like that. They might donate items to be recycled or give money to someplace, but I can't imagine my mom, especially, getting her hands dirty and stinky!"

"I told you—*100 Ways My Father Tortured Me*!" Liling laughed. "I hear my father's voice telling me things I can do, or should do, or don't do, sometimes. I want him to be proud of me, and I think I can—I *will*—do a good job."

Resources

The Classroom Bookshelf
www.theclassroombookshelf.com/?s=motivation

Created by three inspiring teacher-educators, this comprehensive resource is a treasure for anyone who enjoys children's literature. Sponsored by the School Library Journal—the premier resource for language and literacy—this website features blog entries on numerous topics of interest to children, families, educators, and others. The blog authors have also thoughtfully tagged the blogs into searchable categories, so families who wish to read books that can motivate their children may choose from biographies (e.g., *Miss Moore thought Otherwise: How Anne Carroll Moore Created Libraries for Children*), fiction offerings (e.g., *Before Morning; Clayton Byrd Goes Underground*), and other genres.

National Health & Education Center
www.naspcenter.org/parents/earlychildmotiv_ho.html

This web resource provides caregivers and educators with information about motivation for children, particularly focused on learning. The site features links to publications and additional resources as well as connections to the broader umbrella organization, the National Association of School Psychologists. Numerous topics are addressed with supporting information for further exploration and application in the classroom and home environments.

Daniel Pink TED Talk: The Puzzle of Motivation
www.ted.com/talks/dan_pink_on_motivation

This TED Talk features speaker Daniel Pink, who poses questions, challenges, and explanations to viewers about the significance of motivation, rewards, and incentives. The applications of his ideas are well suited to the field of business, and the concepts presented are equally relevant to disciplines such as education, psychology, and human development in general.

References

Adler, S.E. (2018, January/February). The power of negativity. *The Atlantic*, 25.

Aspen Institute. (2017). *How learning happens: Supporting students' social, emotional, and academic development.*

Briceño, E. (2015). Growth mindset: Clearing up some common confusions. *Mind/Shift.* Retrieved from https://www.kqed.org/mindshift/42769/growth-mindset-clearing-up-some-common-confusions

Clark, T. (2011). *Nerve: Poise under pressure, serenity under stress, and the brave new science of fear and cool.* New York, NY: Little, Brown and Company.

Csikszentmihalyi, M. (2008). *Flow: The psychology of optimal experience.* New York, NY: HarperCollins Publishers.

Dweck, C.S. (2016). *Mindset: The new psychology of success.* New York, NY: Ballantine Books.

Dweck, C.S., & Leggett, E.L. (1988). A social-cognitive approach to motivation and personality. *Psychological Review, 95*(2), 256–273.

Gardner, D. (2008). *The science of fear: Why we fear the things we shouldn't-and put ourselves in greater danger.* New York, NY: Dutton.

Hallinan, J.T. (2009). *Why we make mistakes: How we look at things without seeing, forget things in seconds, and are all pretty sure we are way above average.* New York, NY: Broadway Books.

Kohn, A. (1999). *Punished by rewards: The trouble with gold stars, incentive plans, A's, praise, and other bribes.* New York, NY: Houghton Mifflin Harcourt Publishing Company.

Kohn, A. (2017). *Do we perform better under pressure? Exploring unexpected complications and hidden value judgements in a common question.* Retrieved from www.alfiekohn.org/blogs/pressure/

Lepper, M.R., Greene, D., & Nisbett, R.E. (1973). Undermining children's intrinsic interest with extrinsic reward: A test of the "overjustification" hypothesis. *Journal of Personality & Social Psychology, 28*(1), 129–137.

Newberg, A., & Waldman, M.R. (2006). *Why we believe what we believe: Uncovering our biological need for meaning, spirituality, and truth.* New York, NY: Free Press.

Norem, J.K., & Cantor, N. (1986, December). Defensive pessimism. *Journal of Personality and Social Psychology, 51*(6), 1208–1217.

Pink, D.H. (2009). *Drive: The surprising truth about what motivates us.* New York, NY: Riverhead Books.

Rodriguez, V., & Fitzpatrick, M. (2014). *The teaching brain: An evolutionary trait at the heart of education.* New York, NY: The New Press.

Sesamestreet. (2018, February 9). *Dream big, stay motivated, and you could be at the #WinterOlympics one day! #ELMOtivation* [Twitter

Post]. Retrieved from https://twitter.com/sesamestreet/status/962053500019515392

Tolman, E.C. (1948). Cognitive maps in rats and men. *Psychological Review, 55,* 189–208.

Tversky, A., & Kahneman, D. (1974). Judgment under uncertainty: Heuristics and biases. *Science, 185*(4157), 1124–1131.

Yashima, T. (1976). *Crow boy.* New York, NY: Picture Puffins.

5

Risk Factors: Poverty and the Environment

The protagonist in Sherman Alexie's (2007) novel *The Absolutely True Diary of a Part-Time Indian* is Junior—a high school student who faces challenges at home on the Spokane Indian Reservation as well as in the school he attends in Reardon, Washington. Junior eventually overcomes many of these challenges, learning important lessons and losing some childhood innocence along the way. In this story, a teacher— Mr. P—plays an instrumental role in setting Junior on a path that might well lead him out of assured poverty toward self-actualization and a life with, simply put, more choices. This relationship between student and teacher is very brief in the novel, but quite significant, and it captures precisely the significance that Werner and Smith's (2001) research revealed about resilience in that one person can make a tremendous difference in the life of an individual. This is reiterated in much of the literature about child development:

> In a highly significant study that summarized a vast body of child development research, the authors note that, "The essential features of the environment that influence children's development are their relationships with the important people in their lives . . . within the places to which they are exposed— from playgrounds to libraries to schools to soccer fields."
>
> (National Scientific Council on the Developing Child, 2004, p. 4)

As we explore the impact of poverty and the environment on children's development, elements that support a child's capacity to develop qualities that will buffer them against adversity will be explained in the context of the classroom as well as the broader community.

Definitions and Perspectives

Despite a decline in child poverty from 2015 to 2016 (19.7% in 2015 compared with 18% in 2016)—a difference of approximately one million children—children continue to be the poorest age group in the United States (Children's Defense Fund, 2017). To provide some perspective, there were 13,253,000 children living in poverty in the United States in 2016. This number is greater than *the entire population* of the state of Pennsylvania (12,805,537) in 2017, though less than *the entire population* of the state of New York (19,849,399) in 2017. Poverty is defined as "an **annual income below $24,563** for an average family of four" in the United States (Children's Defense Fund, 2017), which equates to approximately $472 a week to cover food, shelter, clothing, electricity, heat, and other expenses for this same family of four.

This same report by the Children's Defense Fund (2017) notes that the highest poverty rates affect the youngest children. In 2016, for example, the number of children living in "extreme poverty" (annual income of **$12,282** for a family of four) was 1,868,000—nearly half of all children under the age of 5 were living in extreme poverty, or approximately one out of every ten children under the age of 5. Additional factors to emphasize include the fact that approximately 8.7 million poor children lived in single-parent families in 2016, and there is a disproportionate number of children identified in census reports as Black and Hispanic who suffer from poverty.

It is interesting to notice how the term "low-income" has become an adjective to describe children and families as opposed to an economic situation. For example, children fitting a specific description are often referred to as "low-income children," and geographic locations are denoted as "low-income communities." It is important to be aware of language that puts people second and attributes first. This can be empowering in some cases, and devaluing and dehumanizing in others.

In the United States, different messages are sent—implicitly and explicitly—about poverty and people who live at or below the poverty line. Consider how poverty is depicted in various media outlets, ranging from fictional television programs to news programs or social media messages. All people are subject to forming beliefs and opinions about poverty, as they are about every other aspect of life. For example, the quote that opens this chapter illustrates a concept that psychologists call "confirmation bias." In this case, this means that beliefs are formed about poverty, and once these beliefs are in place,

> we screen what we see and hear in a biased way that ensures our beliefs are "proven" correct. Psychologists have also discovered that people are vulnerable to something called group polarization—which means that when people who share beliefs get together in groups, they become more convinced that their beliefs are right and they become more extreme in their views. Put confirmation bias, group polarization, and culture together, and we start to understand why people can come to completely different views about which risks are frightening and which aren't worth a second thought.
>
> (Gardner, 2008, p. 15)

Why is this important? As mentioned in Chapter 1, "fundamental attribution error" refers to our tendency to overlook the effects of the social environment on human development and achievement. When children are born into poverty, or become poor due to circumstances that they cannot control, they are vulnerable. And since children are already our most vulnerable citizens due to their size, their age, and the limits of their strength, skills, and knowledge, it is the responsibility of every other able citizen to ensure that their fundamental needs (and rights!) are supported. The sections that follow will focus on specific perspectives that contribute to a fuller understanding of the impact of poverty and the environment on children's learning and development, and how teachers of young children can work together with families and community partners to break the cycle of disadvantage.

Economics

In the 20th century, the "American dream" existed as part of a national, cultural ethos that essentially boiled down to hard work, ambition, and persistence as the keys to success on a pathway out of poverty. These pathways worked differently for White people than people of color, to be sure, yet there were more opportunities for unskilled laborers to find employment. In the 21st century, an economic shift toward occupations in high-technology fields and the service industries has resulted in a gap with firmer—and widening—boundaries separating different socioeconomic classes.

Contributing to the gap is the fact that children and adolescents living in poverty have less access to higher education opportunities, which means that they have fewer opportunities to enter many professions, businesses, and trades that require a specific learned skill set. Underscoring this inequity is the reality that public preK-12 schools in economically disadvantaged communities typically receive fewer resources, attract less qualified teachers and administrators, and therefore contribute less to improving residents' most basic economic situations. "Saying that our economic future rests on the success of our schools while ignoring the connection between our schools and the daily lives of people living in poverty is fundamentally dishonest" (Coleman-Kiner, 2011, p. 25).

Researchers have warned that in a society where, on average, only one out of every ten American kindergarteners living in low-income environments becomes a college graduate (Darling-Hammond, 2010), the U.S. education system simply will not be able to compete on a global scale. And yet those who sit in positions of power and/or privilege in society directly and discreetly benefit from the system that keeps some segments of the society oppressed, as educator Paulo Freire (2014) noted in his writings about class and pedagogy.

Some economic researchers have attempted to quantify the societal damage that occurs due to social inequities, including costs related to increased social spending and lost or diminished economic productivity. For example, in recent research focused on violence against children, authors "estimated the lifetime economic costs of new cases of child abuse in the United States at $124 billion. The calculation included lifetime costs of $210,012 per abuse victim who survived and $1.3 million per victim who died" (Geoghan, 2017, p. 22) and (Fang, Brown, Florence, & Mercy, 2012).

Looking through a lens that considered connections within American society, authors Christakis and Fowler (2009) posit that "understanding the way we are connected is an essential step in creating a more just society and in implementing policies affecting everything from public health to the economy" (p. 32). They provide a simple analogy to explain the relationship between social networks and economic in/equity:

> A person with many friends may become rich and then attract even more friends. This rich-get-richer dynamic means social networks can dramatically reinforce two different kinds of

inequality in our society: *situational inequality* (some are better off socioeconomically) and *positional inequality* (some are better off in terms of where they are located in the network).

(p. 31)

It is often no accident that some children survive and thrive while others suffer, that some children experience joy in learning and others don't, and that some children are provided protections while others are not. "Lost childhoods are a result of choices that exclude particular groups of children by design or neglect. Millions of children have their childhoods cut short because of who they are and where they live" (Geoghan, 2017, p. 1). If we believe this to be true, then we must examine the systems that perpetuate these realities.

Politics

For the purposes of this chapter, the political lens will focus on educational politics, as the broader political systems embedded in American democracy are beyond the scope of this book. However, it is important to note that this is not a new dilemma—indeed, our country has been struggling with the role of politics in education for decades. In my yellowed copy of *Radical School Reform* (Gross & Gross, 1969), I recently reread the editors' introduction, in which they contextualize critics' critiques of schools, stating, "What they find in the classroom is suppression, irrelevance, inhumanity, manipulation, and the systematic stultification of most of what is promising in children and youth" (p. 17).

Some argue that schools are places to transmit culture, with particular effort made to close cultural gaps that lead to academic inequities (Wilson & Weiner, 2001). These cultural gaps (e.g., achievement gap, school-readiness gap) are typically linked to socioeconomic gaps, namely poverty, and the benefits of quality early childhood programs are targeted at reducing our country's high dropout rate. Yet an emphasis on school reform rather than increased, pervasive social services tends to dominate mainstream media attention.

At the time of this writing, Secretary of Education Betsy DeVos had recently participated in a television interview on *60 Minutes* (March 11, 2018). Excerpts from the conversation between interviewer Leslie Stahl and DeVos are provided below:

Stahl: Why take away money from that school that's not working, to bring them up to a level where they are—that school is working?

DeVos: Well, we should be funding and investing in students, not in school—school buildings, not in institutions, not in systems.

Stahl: Okay. But what about the kids who are back at the school that's not working? What about those kids?

***

DeVos: We have invested billions and billions and billions [in public education] from the federal level, and we have seen zero results.

Stahl: But that really isn't true. Test scores have gone up over the last 25 years. So why do you keep saying nothing's been accomplished?

(Blake, 2018)

As the highest education official in the United States, a secretary of education is expected to articulate policy positions clearly, with the educational knowledge and data to support her assertions. The fact that DeVos's appointment was heavily contested during her confirmation hearings was underscored during the interview in which she did not answer questions intelligently or compassionately. One platform that she did continue to emphasize, and which has been in the spotlight in recent years, involves the issue of school choice.

School Choice

The political arguments about school choice stress several important points. Those in favor of school choice argue that families should be allowed to choose the schools that they deem best for their children. The choices may include schools within or outside of their geographical districts and can include public schools and specialized "magnet schools," as well as publicly sponsored, privately managed charter schools. Those against school choice emphasize that not every family has the means to leave a poorly performing school, and "failing" schools would continue to lose funding as students flee to other schools. Furthermore, opponents of school choice believe that inequities would become even greater, and more entrenched. As has been argued in this chapter in the sections above, it becomes increasingly important to consider whose interests are served by sustaining systems that privilege some while harming others. Educator and author Alfie Kohn (2014) asks the penetrating question: "Whose interests are served by the astonishing position that 'no antipoverty tool' . . . is more valuable than an effort to train poor kids to persist at whatever they've been told to do?" (Kohn, 2014). We turn next to considering education and the environments that the educational system creates for young children.

Education

In a recent interview, Linda Cliatt-Wayman, former principal of Strawberry Mansion High School in North Philadelphia, stated:

> Do not fall into this trap of "But you know, they just can't do it. They're poor, they don't have this at home, they don't have that at home. I'm not going to give them that assignment because many of them just can't do it." They can do everything everybody else can do if you expect it and teach it. So, I would always tell my teachers, "I need you to do one thing: teach."
>
> (McKibben, 2018, p. 4)

Cliatt-Wayman's words reflect the notion of growth mindset discussed in the previous chapter, specifically emphasizing the belief that children can increase their potential with the right supports, and that teachers are the most obvious and influential support in any classroom. In a national study of students in Chile, researchers found that students' mindsets were correlated with their standardized test scores. Specifically, students from families experiencing economic challenges "were less likely to hold a growth mindset than their more affluent peers." However, for students identified as having a growth mindset, "it worked as a buffer against the negative effects of poverty on achievement" (Schwartz, 2016, par. 2).

When students in Chile take national exams measuring language and math, they are required to fill out an extensive survey from the Ministry of Education, which covers a range of topics, such as nutrition, bullying, and sports. In 2012, doctoral student Susana Claro convinced the ministry to include two questions related to growth mindset. She stated, "We don't really know if changing mindsets of students is possible at a larger scale and how to work with teachers." She noted that even when teachers are well intentioned, they might be sending messages to students, conveyed directly—or indirectly through the classroom environment—that don't promote a growth mindset or empowerment.

The fact that students who are economically disadvantaged face greater challenges in school is not new information. Students in this situation "are far less likely than their wealthier peers to attend or

graduate college," and the message to students is often a simple one—
"work harder" (Gordon, 2015, par. 1) Critics note that our (U.S.) society
spends the most money educating the wealthiest people. "The people
who need help the most are the most disadvantaged. They end up
going to the universities that spend the smallest amount per student"
(Gordon, 2015, par. 19). The result is that children find themselves in
an educational cycle that extends to their work lives and family lives,
and eventually to society as a whole.

Recognizing that one teacher cannot single-handedly change an
entire societal network of systems, it is inspirational to bring attention to individuals such as Mr. Colbert Nembhard, who created a
library in the Crotona Inn homeless shelter in the Bronx, NY. His goal
is to make reading and exploring books a constant in the lives of children who experience transition more than stability (Stewart, 2016).
Similarly, educators note that "[t]he environment is the curriculum.
Fix that, and we can leave young children to thrive" (Christakis, 2016,
p. 298).

If a learning environment is prepared thoughtfully, with consideration of children's needs and potential, teachers

> won't have to break educational objectives into bite-sized
> pieces; we can feed a child a whole meal. We don't have to
> continually poke and prod and monitor and assess young chil-
> dren. We don't have to harass their teachers and parents either.
> It's the learning environment that needs the continual quality
> assessment, and it's the environment, not the [children] inhab-
> iting it, that needs correcting if found wanting.
>
> (pp. 297–298)

Some fundamental elements related to child development and children's learning can be summarized in terms of several key concepts:

- ◆ Learning is dynamic and changes over time
- ◆ Learning is both cognitive and emotional
- ◆ Learning is context dependent: some children will learn better
  in certain situations, with certain supports, and learn less well
  in others
- ◆ Learning is interactive: it is a social enterprise that happens
  in concert with a variety of active factors in the learner's
  environment, including teachers, parents, peers, textbooks,
  apps, and so on

(Rodriguez, & Fitzpatrick, 2014, p. 51)

When consideration of the classroom environment and understanding of children's learning are focused on children first, the likelihood that they will persist despite obstacles and work toward meaningful goals increases, as does their sense of purpose.

Social and Emotional Competence

"Educating children gives the next generation the tools to fight poverty and prevent disease. It builds confidence, literacy, and dignity. It builds a stronger foundation for the future we all share. And it's every child's right" (Geoghan, 2017, p. 8). This belief is echoed in the words of former principal Cliatt-Wayman, quoted earlier with respect to teachers' beliefs in all children's potential, in spite of poverty or economic status. When a school principal, the educational "leader" of a school building and all that happens within it, articulates strong values about children and how they are perceived, it has an impact on everything and everyone who enters that environment. Cliatt-Wayman said in her interview:

> [I]t was important for me to let those students know that you are not walking around this world unloved. I'm here for you every day, the staff is here for you every day, and we absolutely love you. And we're going to show you that we love you in these ways: we're going to have high expectations for you, we're going to make sure you have the best teacher in the classroom possible, and we're going to make school fun. It was something that they latched on to. They *needed* to hear that they were loved.
>
> (McKibben, 2018, p. 4)

The relationships that are formed between educators and children and families have a lasting effect on children's social and emotional development. Simply knowing children's names and greeting them at the door each morning or in the hallway during the day forges bonds that increase their comfort and their self-esteem. It also lays the vital groundwork for trust that proves invaluable when children are able to share concerns about safety—their own or that of other students—with adults in a classroom or school environment.

There are also benefits of exposing children to the natural surroundings in their community, *outside* of the school building. Becoming more comfortable in their environment contributes to children's appreciation and care for that environment. It is important to note that not all neighborhoods promote safe environments that teachers feel comfortable exploring with the students that they teach, and it is important to notice bias inherent in claims about getting children "out into nature." Researchers have noted that "greener neighborhoods with more trees have many fewer incidences of violence" and residents "also report lower levels of anxiety and outright fear, and much less public and private incivility" (Slade, 2012, p. 246). The case study at the end of this chapter provides an example of teachers who found ways to bring their students into their urban school setting, as well as to visit places outside the immediate surroundings, and the impact that was evident in the children's learning and motivation.

Safe Spaces

As educators strive to motivate children to learn and take risks that ultimately increase joy and understanding, it is increasingly challenging for teachers to maintain an optimistic stance toward education when schools are portrayed as unsafe, potentially dangerous places where the threat of violence supplants joy in learning and exploration. The following quote is particularly apt in relation to the concepts of grit, resilience, and motivation:

> There was a time when children were expected to take some knocks and chances. It was part of growing up. But no more. At schools, doors are barred and guarded against maniacs with guns, while children are taught from their first day in the classroom that every stranger is a threat. In playgrounds, climbing equipment is removed and unsupervised games of tag are forbidden lest someone sprain an ankle or bloody a nose. At home, children are forbidden from playing alone outdoors, as all generations did before, because their parents are convinced every bush hides a pervert—and no mere statistic will convince them otherwise. Childhood is starting to resemble a prison sentence, with children spending almost every moment behind locked doors and alarms, their every movement scheduled, supervised, and controlled. Are they at least safer as a result? Probably not. Obesity, diabetes, and the other health problems caused in part by too much time sitting

inside are a lot more dangerous than the specters haunting
parental imaginations.

(Gardner, 2008, p. 12)

How, then, can teachers of young children create spaces where children and families feel welcome and safe?

Classrooms can be thoughtfully designed to reflect the children
who learn there, including their families and elements from the surrounding community. For example, systematic communication with
families, through the use of technology tools, paper newsletters, or
documentation (e.g., photos, samples of students' work and conversations), opens access to information and extends the environmental
reach. Boundaries may be co-constructed and maintained in innova-
tive ways that invite input over time. Teachers, administrators, caregivers, and community members can bring energy and expertise to
children's classrooms, underscoring a fundamental value that any
power associated with teaching and learning is strengthened through
collaboration. Many teachers

limit ourselves to considerations of things like music, artifacts,
and food as ways to bring the lives of families into the classroom, holding back from asking parents to collaborate with
us as we arrange our classroom environments, establish daily
rhythms, and make decisions.

(Pelo, 2011, p. 37)

Collaborating with families about environmental considerations cer-
tainly involves challenges, but it also creates opportunities for relationships and new perspectives that can promote learning across contexts.

Simple strategies welcome families and community members into
the classroom and school environments. For example, in one classroom,
teachers placed adult-sized chairs strategically in the learning space,
inviting adults to sit and participate in children's activities. In doing
so, teachers intentionally sent out a message of "welcome" to parents,
letting the classroom arrangement convey the teachers' appreciation
for observations and interpretation. Teachers invited multiple perspectives that sometimes challenged their thinking and sparked new
curriculum, conversations, and avenues for inquiry. Interactions of
this sort support the development of new relationships and strengthen
school communities (Hilliard, 2011). In the chapter that follows, we
will focus on the role of differences and diversity in the classroom and
how these contribute to children's development.

Turning Ideas Into Action

Classroom Store

Goal: To introduce children to the concept of paying for items and to raise awareness about the costs and challenges associated with having sufficient funds to get (1) what we want, (2) what we need, or (3) what we can afford

Materials needed: A dramatic play area in the classroom that can be transformed into a store. If there is no such area, then creating a dedicated space for the store of choice will be needed. This area should have features of a store, such as shelves or a few tables where items can be displayed, as well as a cash register/checkout area where children will bring their items.

Action: Based on the children's current interests, discuss as a group the type of store that the classroom will feature for a while. For example, if the children wish to have a grocery store in their classroom, that is a classic example that affords lots of options. If children are interested in a pet store or a flower store or a computer store, these ideas are as wonderful as many others in terms of the creativity that is engendered through discussion and preparations.

Once the type of store has been determined, groups of children can take responsibility for "stocking" the store. Children may bring in items from their families, teachers can take responsibility for stocking the store in advance, or children may draw, paint, or otherwise create the items they wish to feature. The choices are limitless. What is required is that price tags are placed on each individual item. While it might not be realistic in terms of real-world shopping, for the purposes of this activity try to keep prices of items at $1.00 or less.

When all items have been created/found, priced, and placed in the store, then the exercise can begin. Tell the children that they have $5.00 to spend in the store. Depending on the type of store, the children may want or need different items, and regardless of the type of store, they will only be able to afford a limited number of items. The math concepts and operations are not the primary focus here—there will be plenty of time for them to practice these skills. The primary focus is the discussion that emerges from the challenge of having enough money to obtain what you want. What is the difference between getting what you want and what you need? And what happens if what you want or need is not something you can afford? Discuss with children the notion of having "enough" money. What supports exist for people who do not have enough money to buy what they want or need?

Figure 5.1 Class Store 1

Extension: A field trip to a local bank, or a visit from a parent or community member who works in a bank or social service agency, can be informative for children. The group may wish to collect spare change from family members or school personnel that they will donate to a chosen organization, perhaps one that contributes food or other amenities to children and families.

Figure 5.2 Class Store 2

Gratitude Garden

Goal: To identify concrete and abstract elements of the children's daily lives that they are grateful for, and to encourage awareness about inequity

Materials needed: Construction paper of different colors; scissors; glue sticks or glue; magazines or other print materials (e.g., wrapping paper, newspaper)

Action: Discuss with children the concept of a garden—what is a garden? What do you find in a garden? How do we take care of a garden? Discuss the concept of gratitude—what are some things that we are grateful for in our lives? Children can share their ideas about things and/or people in their lives for which they are grateful.

Invite the children to create their own garden, which will represent things that they are grateful for and will communicate this gratitude to others. The children can discuss and decide upon an area in the classroom that will serve as the garden, such as a wall space, an area or "center" in the classroom, or a hallway area (e.g., on or around cubbies, bulletin board). Children can then populate the garden with items that represent what they are grateful for. For example, they can draw a picture in the center of a flower depicting the item for which or the person for whom they are grateful. They may wish to glue or draw an image on a flower-like template that you provide, and then these flowers can be "planted" in the garden by either taping the flowers to a wall or using Styrofoam packing materials as the ground into which sticks/stems can be poked.

The types of things that you see children drawing/depicting will provide you with an opportunity to extend conversation and stretch their thinking. For example, if a student draws a picture of her pink towel and says that she is grateful for the towel because it is soft and she uses it when she bathes, that is different from feeling grateful for a toy or a video game. Conversation can include feeling grateful for food, shelter, loved ones, and more. Similar to the store activity described earlier, this activity also raises distinctions between what we want, need, and can afford or have access to. This activity presents children with an opportunity to notice and identify inequities in what people may want and what they may not be able to acquire or experience. This motivation translates nicely into efforts to help people who may not receive what they need, and it shows how children can help provide simple things (e.g., messages, kind gestures) that make a difference in the lives of others, while addressing inequities as a group.

Nature Mural

Goal: To get outside! To encourage children to notice aspects of their environment in a new way, and to engage with nature in its various forms.

Materials needed: Large piece of paper upon which to create the nature mural—this can be paper from a large roll of paper (e.g., 4 feet long) or else several pieces of paper connected together with tape or staples to make a progressive mural (e.g., paper shopping bags cut and connected, individual sheets of paper or newspaper); glue or glue sticks; tape; markers or crayons; digital cameras or cell phones with cameras

Figure 5.3 Nature Mural

to take pictures of the surroundings and the numerous elements found within the surroundings

Action: Discuss the idea of taking a nature walk with the children. Depending on the location of your classroom and school, the options will vary. Even schools in the most densely packed urban environment will have spaces to explore. For example, if you decide to walk around the city block, what do you notice about the ground upon which you are walking? Is the ground concrete? Asphalt? Dirt? Bringing paper and pencils or crayons presents an opportunity for children to do rubbings of the ground surface, as well as a building's surface. Where do you notice green space, trees, plants, flowers, and/or animals? As you are walking, encourage the children to notice nature along the way. Are there flower petals or leaves that have fallen on the ground? Encourage children to collect several items that they can bring back to the classroom and glue onto the mural or recreate through their own drawing/painting on the mural.

If there are no flowers or plants in the near vicinity, are there stores (e.g., florist, market) that sell flowers or plants? Ask a shop employee if the children may come inside and examine these items using their senses—how do these items look, smell, feel? If there is a park or other green space nearby, what types of foliage capture their attention? What animals or other creatures are visible? Invite children to share with each other their ideas about what is interesting, curious, and so on. When the children are ready to create their nature mural, they can discuss and decide how to represent what they saw and what they gathered while on their walk. They may choose to work together or alone on this project, and you may guide them accordingly. The finished mural may be displayed inside the classroom or in the hallway, inviting others to notice and interpret the surroundings as represented by the children and making use of unique features of the classroom space.

Extension: Based on the experience, children may develop questions and/or ideas about what they would like to see in their environment. For example, they may wish there were more trees or flowers in their neighborhood or more animals to see and learn about. If it is possible to bring some of these items into the classroom, that is one possibility, and another option is to investigate what it would take to plant a tree in a neighborhood space. Contacting town hall or city government officials is one way to begin to learn about the options for children in your class to add something to their natural surroundings.

A Closer Look: Poverty and the Environment

The students in the Cypress Tree preschool classroom consistently encountered natural materials in their daily play. Ms. Abby and Mr. Micah, teachers trained in the Waldorf and Montessori approaches, respectively, believed that natural, beautiful materials, such as wood and sand, engage students and convey to them that their work is important and special. Within the urban classroom they shared, Ms. Abby and Mr. Micah set up a nature area, which changed with every topic that they focused on in their curriculum. Every fall, for example, they incorporated acorns, different varieties of leaves, pinecones, apples, root vegetables, and pumpkins into their nature space. The students enjoyed learning about the fall season, so the teachers decided to plan a nature walk that the class would take around their neighborhood. If someone had asked either Ms. Abby or Mr. Micah to describe the neighborhood surrounding their school, neither of them would have used the words "safe" or "pretty" in their responses. In fact, both teachers suspected the students felt this same way, too. Ms. Abby sometimes felt a little blue, almost as if there was a gray cloud hanging over her workplace.

A few weeks before the planned nature walk, the class of 16 students went on a field trip to an apple orchard several miles from their school. While at the orchard, the students and teachers rode the hayride, picked apples, drank freshly pressed apple cider that they helped to press, and ate cider donuts, fresh out of the baker's oven. The students were so excited about that field trip that Ms. Abby and Mr. Micah were that much more revved up to get outside and explore their own backyard, so to speak. Most of the children lived in the building complex near the elementary school, and almost half of the children's families could be classified as "low-income." The teachers knew that at least two children had been living in transitional housing with their families because the adults couldn't afford the rent prices in the area. Their urban environment didn't have many open spaces or green spaces, so the children weren't used to seeing "nature" in their everyday lives. This was one of the main reasons why Ms. Abby and Mr. Micah were particularly committed to integrating the outdoors with their indoor classroom environment day after day.

***

After snack time, the teachers gathered the students on the carpet and explained how their nature walk would begin. They brainstormed some rules that the group would follow, such as "No running or pushing" and "Make sure you can always see a teacher!" They paired students up with one another to form nature buddies and brought out the rope that the children would hold on to with one hand the entire time the class was walking. In their other hand the students carried brown paper lunch bags that contained plastic magnifying glasses that the children could use to examine more closely the objects that they noticed. Mr. Micah explained to the children that they were encouraged to touch, smell, listen to, and look at the natural world around them once they got outside. If the children found and were intrigued by natural objects (e.g., leaves, pebbles, sticks) that they found on the ground, the teachers explained to them that they could pick those up and put them into their paper bags. Ms. Abby excitedly told the group that they would use these materials to make fairy houses that afternoon. The students gasped and said "Oooh!" appreciatively.

Once outside, the children first wanted to stop and pick up every leaf and twig they came across, thereby stopping every few feet to examine and pack away their findings. Ms. Abby and Mr. Micah smiled to each other as they listened to the children's conversations:

"Look at this!"

"What is THAT?"

"Let's get the magnifying glass!"

"That smells good!"

After walking for 15 minutes, the teachers told the students that they would take a break. They walked over to the nearest reasonable place to stop and examine their artifacts. They chose the bus stop since there was a bench and students could gather all around that bench, as opposed to standing in front of one another, trying to see and talk with friends. During the break, some students began drawing in the dirt using sticks they'd gathered on their walk. Others were engaged in dramatic play, using characters from that morning's "read aloud." Ms. Abby entered into their conversations, asking them what the students in class would use to make their fairy houses. The students looked in their bags to remind themselves and share all of the items that they had collected, and they began creating plans. No one had ever seen a fairy house close up before, though Kayla emphatically stated she used to have one in her window "before the windy came."

***

After naptime, Mr. Micah shared a book about fairy houses that he'd borrowed from the local library. He showed the group how he'd placed a few other books at the different tables that he and Ms. Abby had set up while the children dozed. These, he said, could be used for inspiration. Along with the books, the teachers put out clay that had been donated by the landscaping company that Marco's uncle worked for, as well as work trays that featured an assortment of tools—metal forks and spoons, clear fishing line, colored yarn, wooden toothpicks, and buttons that the teachers had collected over time. Children were invited to get their paper bags from their cubbies to begin working on their fairy houses.

As the children worked, they freely shared their ideas and opinions with each other:

"Luca, you could add a window here so your fairies can see outside."

"If your clay starts to crack, use a little bit of water on your pinky to dab it."

"Remember, there's no rush to finish!"

Ms. Abby walked over to Kayla and asked her how she felt making her fairy house. Though Kayla continued working, she turned her face up to look at Ms. Abby—smiling so that her nose crinkled and her eyes glimmered.

"Ms. Abby, my love light is shining!"

In that moment, Ms. Abby and Mr. Micah decided to make a nature walk a regular part of every month's activities. Over the years, the preschool students witnessed seasons changing, neighborhood structures rising and being taken down, and community members turning from strangers into friends of the school. Neighborhood business owners noticed the students on their walks and donated items to the school to be used in play and future explorations. From time to time, when Ms. Abby and Mr. Micah felt particularly happy about a lesson or an interaction with a child and/or caregiver, they would turn to the other—sometimes from across the room—and make an "L" shape with their thumb and forefingers, which forever conveyed the enthusiastic and heartfelt sentiment, "My love light is shining!"

Figure 5.4 Fairy House

Resources

Child in the City

www.childinthecity.org/

Child in the City is an organization that brings together professionals and practitioners in a variety of fields with the goal of promoting children's rights and well-being in countries around the world. Through articles, blogs, and conferences, Child in the City supports collaboration among citizens of all ages, as well as the overall development of high-quality pedagogy and practice.

National Center for Children in Poverty

www.nccp.org/topics/childpoverty.html

For over 25 years the NCCP has been a tremendous resource for anyone interested in learning about how poverty affects children's development, both in the moment and across the life span. The organization's website provides links to comprehensive reports, projects, and more in an effort to raise awareness and inspire action.

UNICEF Child-Friendly Cities

https://childfriendlycities

This website provides visitors with vital information about UNICEF's commitment to promoting and supporting child-friendly communities. This work grew out of the Convention on the Rights of the Child, endorsed by members of the United Nations. Case studies, current research, and criteria for action plans demonstrate citizens' efforts and initiatives.

References

Alexie, S. (2007). *The absolutely true diary of a part-time Indian*. New York, NY: Little, Brown and Company.

Aspen Institute. (2017). *How learning happens: Supporting students' social, emotional, and academic development.*

Blake, A. (2018). Betsy DeVos's botched "60 Minutes" interview, annotated. *The fix: Analysis*. Retrieved from www.washingtonpost.com/news/the-fix/wp/2018/03/12/betsy-devoss-botched-60-minutes-interview-annotated/?utm_term=.23db906d5cdd

Children's Defense Fund. (2017). Child poverty. *The State of America's Children*. Retrieved from www.childrensdefense.org/library/state-of-americaschildren/documents/Child_Poverty.pdf

Christakis, E. (2016). *The importance of being little: What preschoolers really need from grownups*. New York, NY: Viking.

Christakis, N.A., & Fowler, J.H. (2009). *Connected: How your friends' friends' friends affect everything you feel, think, and do*. New York, NY: Back Bay Books.

Coleman-Kiner, A. (2011, June 8). Leading with love. *Education Week, 30*(33), 25.

Darling-Hammond, L. *The flat world and education: How America's commitment to equity will determine our future*. New York: Teachers College Press.

Fang, X., Brown, D.S., Florence, C.S., & Mercy, J.A. (2012). The economic burden of child maltreatment in the United States and implications for prevention. *Child Abuse & Neglect, 36*(2), 156–165.

Freire, P. (2014). *Pedagogy of the oppressed: 30th anniversary edition*. New York, NY: Bloomsbury Academic.

Gardner, D. (2008). *The science of fear: Why we fear the things we shouldn't-and put ourselves in greater danger*. New York, NY: Dutton.

Geoghan, T. (2017). *Stolen childhoods: End of childhood report 2017*. Fairfield, CT: Save the Children.

Gordon, T. (2015). Telling poor, smart kids that all it takes is hard work to be as successful as their wealthy peers is a blatant lie. *Atlanta Black Star*. Retrieved from http://atlantablackstar.com/2015/06/03/telling-poor-smart-kids-takes-hard-work-successful-wealthy-peers-blatant-lie/

Gross, R., & Gross, B. (Eds.). (1969). *Radical school reform*. New York: Simon & Schuster.

Hilliard, D. (2011). Making families welcome. *Environments: A beginnings workshop book* (pp. 44–45). Redmond, WA: Exchange Press, Inc.

Kohn, A. (2014). *Grit: A skeptical look at the latest educational fad*. Retrieved from www.alfiekohn.org/article/grit/

McKibben, S. (2018). Push, don't pity, students in poverty. *Education Update*, *60*(1), 1, 4–5.

National Scientific Council on the Developing Child (NSCDC). (2004). *Young children develop in an environment of relationships*. Working Paper No. 1. Retrieved from www.developingchild.net

Pelo, A. (2011). From borders to bridges: Transforming our relationships with parents. *Environments: A beginnings workshop book* (pp. 37–40). Redmond, WA: Exchange Press, Inc.

Rodriguez, V., & Fitzpatrick, M. (2014). *The teaching brain: An evolutionary trait at the heart of education*. New York, NY: The New Press.

Schwartz, K. (2016). A growth mindset could buffer kids from negative academic effects of poverty. *Mind/Shift*. Retrieved from ww2.kqed.org/mindshift/2016/07/26/a-growth-mindset-could-buffer-kids-from-negative-academic-effects-of-poverty/

Slade, G. (2012). *The big disconnect: The story of technology and loneliness*. New York, NY: Prometheus Books.

Stewart, N. (2016, November 24). A Bronx librarian keen on teaching homeless children a lasting love of books. *The New York Times*. Retrieved from www.nytimes.com/2016/11/24/nyregion/a-bronx-librarian-keen-on-teaching-homeless-children-a-lasting-love-of-books.html

Werner, E.E., & Smith, R.S. (2001). *Journeys from childhood to midlife: Risk, resilience, and recovery*. Ithaca, NY: Cornell University Press.

Wilson, D.M. & Weiner, R. (2001, October 10). Education called key to defense. *[Rockland County, NY] Journal News*, p. B1.

6

Risk Factors: Race, Gender, and Disability

Children are aware of the messages sent—deliberately and unintentionally—by peers, family and community members, and the media. They are influenced by these messages in sometimes detrimental ways, and sometimes in ways that give them strength they would otherwise not recognize in themselves. At the time of this writing, some of the more challenging issues that teachers and families report, which are emphasized in a variety of media outlets, include immigration, gender identity and expression, systemic racism, religious prejudice and bias, violence, and terrorism. Teachers of young children often feel conflicted about discussing these topics in class because they worry that families might not agree with their opinions or the school's stance on a particular topic. Their own discomfort with or misconceptions about topics and labels also cause teachers to avoid or ignore questions that children bring into the classroom.

The challenge with this approach is that children ask questions and seek meaning on their own, at unpredictable times as well as in the aftermath of a major event (e.g., political election, natural disaster). Children look to adults in their lives to guide, inform, and validate their thinking. It is therefore important to establish open, two-way relationships with families, and to find out from them how they choose to discuss topics that arise that may be particularly sensitive, provocative, and difficult to discuss without thoughtful, intentional attention.

In a classroom context, the absence of questions about a topic doesn't mean that the children are not curious about it. Establishing a classroom culture where all questions are welcome and answers are arrived at respectfully and collaboratively ensures that children will feel most comfortable verbalizing their own musings and concerns. Author and educator bell hooks maintains that "[t]he unwillingness to approach teaching from a standpoint that includes awareness of race, sex, class, etc., is often rooted in the fear that classrooms will be uncontrollable, that emotions and passions will not be contained" (as cited in Perry & Fraser, 1993, p. 93). The sections and activities that follow in this chapter present terms and topics that can lead to rich classroom (and staff) discussions, and that can provide experiences to anchor discussion for young children's evolving understandings of their world and their role in it.

Definitions and Perspectives

For the purposes of this chapter, the topics of race, gender, and ability will be explored in detail, yet it is important to acknowledge that there are numerous other topics that can create challenges for teachers. These challenges, however, differ significantly from the challenges faced by individuals whose daily lives are impacted by them. The first step toward developing comfort, empathy, and less biased understanding of diversity is to articulate the values that underlie the classroom curriculum and experiences for all children. This is both a philosophical stance and a specific approach to classroom practices. Author bell hooks posits that "most of us were taught in classrooms where styles of teaching reflected the notion of a single norm of thought and experience, which we were encouraged to believe was a universal norm. This has been just as true for non-White teachers as for White teachers" (as cited in Perry & Fraser, 1993, p. 91)

Diversity
Diversity is a term often used, and used in multiple ways, sometimes without a specific definition or goal:

> Sometimes it is used as a euphemism for race or gender in an attempt to soften the impact of discussing racism and sexism directly. At other times, it is used to include practically every human difference under the sun, from smokers to nonsmokers, frozen yogurt to ice cream lovers, and every other

possible variable. It is a term that can mean everything or nothing. Yet, the current attention being given to the issue of diversity is an attempt to answer some fundamental questions about human identity and experience:

Who are we?
What are we?
Whose descriptions define us?
How do those definitions develop and affect us?
Why are our identities important and why should we explore them at all?
How do they impact the way we see ourselves and lead our lives?
Who has access and power and to whom are they denied or restricted?
Why is there such division among people?
How can we come together?

(DeRosa & Johnson, 2002, pp. 1–2)

For hundreds of years, citizens in the United States have struggled with the notion of equality and the biases and prejudices that have developed in American society over time. While some progress in terms of equity and equality has indeed occurred slowly in different pockets of the citizenry, some educators note that "the shift towards greater visibility and inclusion of people previously marginalized in our society also leads to more explicit opposition from people already in the mainstream" (LeeKeenan & Nimmo, 2016, p. 66). As teachers begin their own journeys of self-reflection and awareness of implicit and explicit biases, they also influence children's awareness of practices that support the unfair treatment of any individuals because of their identity.

For example, in the March 2015 issue of *Educational Leadership*, educators focused on cultural diversity in classrooms. Some of the important elements featured in this issue include consideration of facility in several languages as an asset that enhances American society, advocacy, and recognizing that no classroom or curriculum is ever value-neutral. Adapted from a Twitter post by Brandon Johnson, Figure 6.1 illustrates the major themes of the articles in this particular issue, featuring quotes from the authors.

Many parents argue that it is better for children to be raised in an area that has diverse systems in place, and this includes attending a school with a diverse student and family community. When it comes

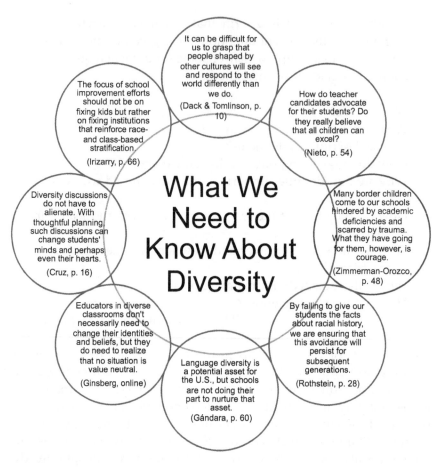

Figure 6.1 Diversity (ASCD image)

to actualizing that goal, however, caregivers sometimes experience a tension accepting what they perceive to be lower educational quality for a higher level of perceived diversity.

Author and parent Nikole Hannah-Jones (2016) describes it this way: "You want it to be multicultural. . . . So we're all living in Brooklyn because we want that to be part of the upbringing. But you can understand how a parent might look at it and go, 'While I want diversity, I don't want profound imbalance'" (par. 76). She also observes what she calls a "carefully curated integration," which "allows many white parents to boast that their children's public schools look like the United Nations, [but] comes at a steep cost for the rest of the city's black and Latino children" (Hannah-Jones, 2016, par. 8). Part of the challenge is that people tend to focus on one aspect of diversity and therefore inflate or diminish that aspect in their efforts to accommodate (or "tolerate") differences. This narrow focus contributes to an inaccurate, incomplete understanding of individuals. "The single story creates stereotypes, and the problem with stereotypes is not that they are untrue, but that they are incomplete. They make one story become the only story" (Adichie, 2009, par. 24). One of the most important concepts that has had tremendous influence in the United States and around the world is that of race, and it remains a primary responsibility of all early childhood educators to find ways to prevent and repair stereotyping and bias in the classroom.

Race

The concept of *race* is not a scientific categorization, and in the biological sense, race does not exist. There is no scientific evidence that groups that have grown out of social organization differ biologically or genetically in more ways than they are alike. In fact, many physical qualities that distinguish people—and contribute to subsequent categorization into racial groups—originated, long ago, as necessary adaptations to environmental contexts. Author Sonia Nieto (2000) stresses that "differences that do exist are primarily social; that is, they are based on one's experiences within a particular cultural group. There is really only one 'race'"—the human race (p. 27). She writes that it is widely understood that "the very concept of race is a social construction, that is, a racial group is socially and not biologically determined" (p. 27).

Racism

The social construction of race has led to racism, which includes people's actions and attitudes as well as the practices that are perpetuated in any societal institution (e.g., school, hospital), particularly when these promote one group's culture or livelihood and simultaneously suppress those of another group.

In a recent class with first-year college students, I showed the video *A Class Divided* (see www.pbs.org/wgbh/frontline/film/class-divided/), which was created in 1985. This video shows one third-grade teacher's attempt to teach students about discrimination in Riceville, Iowa (population ≅ 800), and how her treatment of children based on eye color greatly influenced their self-concepts, their friendships, and their test scores in less than one day. The classroom discussion with college-age students was poignant and powerful—even 33 years after this film was made, and 50 years after Jane Elliott first used this experiment with the students she had the pleasure and responsibility to teach. Discussions about race and racism therefore belong in early childhood classrooms because the earlier a child can counter current and potential damage, the more beneficial it will be for her cognitive, social-emotional, and physical development.

An infographic, such as the one created by early childhood educator Jarrod Fischer Green (2018) in collaboration with other practitioners, is useful to share with colleagues and families: http://www.childrenscommunityschool.org/social-justice-resources/. These types of tools help people understand that from a developmental perspective, young children are more than capable of participating in discussions about race, as well as activities that strengthen their understanding and empathy.

It is also important to acknowledge the particular "difficulties educators of color might face in teaching about race, ethnicity, and privilege, particularly in predominantly white settings" (Webb, 2018, p. 56). As mentioned previously, there are no value-neutral discussions about diversity, and this includes race. Yet people of color are sometimes "suspiciously viewed as having personal agendas" (Webb, 2018, p. 57).

People of Color

What does the term *people of color* mean, specifically? This term evolved as an inclusive category for people who have been labeled "minority" in a society that is predominantly White (e.g., Native Americans, African Americans, Latinos, and Asian Americans), and it implies significant connections and shared/similar lived experiences for many individuals living in the United States. Criticism of and dissatisfaction with this term stems from

> the implication of a common historical experience among all those included under this designation. Aside from a mutual history of oppression at the hands of those in power—not an insignificant commonality—a shared historical experience among all people of color is an illusion. Moreover, a presumed common experience suggests that there is no conflict among these groups. As we know, such conflicts not only exist but they have resulted in periodic outbreaks of serious interethnic violence. These emanate not only from a shared oppression and the competition for scarce resources that results from political domination, but also from deep-seated cultural and social differences among the groups themselves.
>
> (Nieto, 2000, p. 28)

Nieto also cautions against the practice of "lumping groups together." While some groups indeed share many cultural attributes, they also differ in many significant ways.

> A Guatemalan and a Dominican, for example, may both speak Spanish, practice the Catholic religion, and share deeply rooted family values. But the native language of some Guatemalans is not Spanish, and Dominicans have an African background not shared by most Guatemalans. . . . For this reason, I try to refer to each group by national origin. Besides being more accurate, it is ordinarily how people prefer to be called.
>
> (Nieto, 2000, p. 29)

As you grapple with the clumsiness that often accompanies practicing and understanding new ideas, it helps to maintain a focus on equity and empowerment, which are goals that can motivate you to persist in creating a socially just and inclusive classroom environment.

Empowerment

Describing the principal of her daughter's segregated school, author Hannah-Jones (2016) notes that she "rejected the spare educational orthodoxy often reserved for poor black and brown children that strips away everything that makes school joyous in order to focus solely on improving test scores" (par. 15). Children at the school Hannah-Jones describes had violin lessons and learned to speak Mandarin, and the school also received funds from a federal magnet grant that supported a science, technology, engineering, and math (STEM) program. The principal hoped that these offerings would appeal to families whose income placed them in the "middle class," and whose immediate neighborhood school did not offer such valuable content.

Former principal and author Linda Nathan is critical of an educational system that privileges some over others and promises success without necessary supports. She writes, "I have too many students who because of misreading a form, or experiencing a family tragedy, or because of racism or lack of explicit support from their college ended up leaving and owing money for a degree they never got" (Nathan, 2017, p. 9). In order for students and families engaged with any facets of the educational system to be fully empowered, systemic advantages must be recognized and—by some—abandoned in the interest of equity. As we turn to the topic of gender, the poem "Life Doesn't

Frighten Me"[1] by poet Maya Angelou serves as a bridge between two concepts that are socially constructed yet impact all aspects of children's development:

Shadows on the wall
Noises down the hall
Life doesn't frighten me at all

Bad dogs barking loud
Big ghosts in a cloud
Life doesn't frighten me at all

Mean old Mother Goose
Lions on the loose
They don't frighten me at all

Dragons breathing flame
On my counterpane
That doesn't frighten me at all.

I go boo
Make them shoo
I make fun
Way they run
I won't cry
So they fly
I just smile
They go wild

Life doesn't frighten me at all.

Tough guys in a fight
All alone at night
Life doesn't frighten me at all.

Panthers in the park
Strangers in the dark
No, they don't frighten me at all.

That new classroom where
Boys all pull my hair
(Kissy little girls
With their hair in curls)
They don't frighten me at all.

Don't show me frogs and snakes
And listen for my scream,
If I'm afraid at all
It's only in my dreams.

I've got a magic charm
That I keep up my sleeve
I can walk the ocean floor
And never have to breathe.

Life doesn't frighten me at all
Not at all
Not at all.

Life doesn't frighten me at all.

Gender

The speaker in Angelou's poem emphasizes and reiterates the idea that we do not need to fear the many things that we encounter in life. In fact, the speaker, a child, demonstrates her empowerment, scaring off the things that could otherwise defeat her. As a young Black girl, Angelou experienced significant trauma, including her parents' difficult relationship and her own sexual assault at age 8. She became mute for five years following her sexual assault, and she later credited a beloved teacher for helping her reclaim her voice.

Like race, gender is a socially constructed concept, as opposed to sex, which is biologically determined at birth. Gender stereotyping, therefore, refers to generalizations about gender—male, female, or other along a gender spectrum—that are associated with negative or derogatory connotations. Sexism refers to the actions, attitudes, and practices that promote one sex while suppressing another. Recent research about the biology and behavior of humans—and other species—indicates that many of the assumptions that have contributed to societal expectations related to gender are incorrect. For example:

The classic evolutionary explanation of behavioral differences between men and women holds that they reflect an evolved pattern seen across the animal kingdom. Many gender gaps, in this view, are thus "natural." But research has shown that many of the foundational assumptions of this account are wrong. Environmental factors, moreover, can play a key role in the development of evolved behaviors. Progressive cultural shifts do not "go against" nature but rewrite it.

(Fine & Elgar, 2017, p. 34)

Similar to the developmental milestones illustrated in the infographic about race, presented in the previous section, children experience milestones in their understanding and internalizations about gender:

In Western cultures . . . within the first year of life infants begin to distinguish people by sex, seeing individuals as either male or female. By about 18 months toddlers begin to understand gendered words such as "girl" or "man" and associate those words with sex-matched faces. By 24 months children know of sex stereotypes (such as associating women with lipstick) and before their third birthday nearly all kids label themselves and others with gender labels that match their sex.

(Olson, 2017, p. 47)

Early childhood teachers are familiar with the types of play that occur during children's preschool years, in which children often display strong preferences for same-sex peers and repeatedly choose activities typically associated with their sex. During this time, children also tend to show an evolving understanding about their sex, specifically "that girls develop into women and boys into men" (Olson, 2017, p. 47).

Research has shown that transgender girls and boys (children who identify as girls and boys, but at birth were considered to be boys and girls, respectively) predict their identities into the future in the same way—trans girls see themselves becoming women and trans boys believe that they will be men (Olson, 2017).

Transgender Identity and Brain Development

Teachers sometimes experience discomfort when speaking with parents or caregivers of young children whose behavior is different than "typical" play among preschool children. It is helpful to explain that gender identity consists of sexual identity (biological) as well as role identity (social). The two components interact in different ways for different children, and different cultures and environments contribute to children's developing identity. It is therefore important to nurture a classroom environment in which constraints imposed by stereotypes are discouraged and equality is promoted in all activities that contribute to children's holistic development (e.g., cognitive, physical, social-emotional).

Children who make choices about toys and clothes that are gender nonconforming (e.g., girls who want to play with trucks and dress like "tough" superheroes, boys who want to play "princess" and wear sparkly or frilly pink clothing) are not necessarily transgender. Research suggests that the way children talk about their gender identity—feeling you are a girl as opposed to feeling that you wish the world was ok with your being a feminine boy—more likely predicts the different developmental paths of children (Olson, 2017). This has inspired more research with people who have nonbinary identities—they do not feel fully boy or girl, masculine or feminine. They fall somewhere along a spectrum that society is slowly beginning to recognize in new and evolving norms.

Researchers have been searching for genetic and other signs that could explain differences, for example, in the brain development of people who identify as one sex versus another. Complicating this research, however, is the fact that humans' brains actually change in response to experience *and* the environment, so scientists can't be certain whether any brain differences that are identified "*cause* the experience of a particular gender identity or *reflect* the experience of gender identity" (Olson, 2017, p. 48). Author Kristina R. Olson makes an astute statement in her writing, however, that "the most critical questions about transgender children . . . are about their wellbeing" (p. 48). Isn't this at the heart of every teacher's commitment to the children in their care? As we continue to examine closely facets of what it means to be human, we turn now to the human experience of disability.

Disability

Similar to the concepts of race and gender, there are numerous political, cultural, and social constructs related to disability. Unlike race and gender, however, disability is inextricably connected to a child's cognitive and/or physical being. It is therefore compelling to critically consider how teaching young children can contribute to a more socially just society and encourage them to question the power dynamics that exist for children who are disabled.

Disabilities may include intellectual disabilities (e.g., Down syndrome), motor disabilities (e.g., cerebral palsy), sensory impairments (e.g., vision, hearing), speech and language disabilities, and behavioral or emotional challenges. Working with young children in inclusive settings has long been the practice in early childhood education, but laws were not put in place to ensure equitable access to education until fairly recently (specific legislation is addressed later in this chapter).

Teachers of young children are committed to flexibility and creativity in terms of how information is presented, and to providing necessary accommodations and supports for children so that *all children* may work toward developmentally appropriate, high expectations.

For example, teaching strategies can include simple techniques such as labeling areas and items in the classroom, managing noise and human traffic, maintaining levels of lighting that are conducive to learning and not distracting, accessibility to areas and materials in the classroom and around the school, consistency and predictability in the classroom routine (especially transitions), and rules and expectations that are thoughtfully and collaboratively discussed. Considerations also include attending to children's psychological and physical safety. This could include specific areas of the classroom being designated as quiet areas, and intentional planning to encourage children's independent access to materials and curriculum while avoiding overstimulation and disorganization as much as possible. It is important to empower children to cope with negative stereotypes and to counter behaviors such as name calling or navigate physical barriers.

One way to help and support children in this effort is to teach all children to use "people-first" language, or person-first terminology (PFT). This practice is applicable when speaking of children with disabilities, and it is also generalizable to any other situation in which a person is greater than one characteristic or quality that they possess. For example, referring to a child as a "child who is hearing-impaired" places the child ahead of her disability. Similarly, a "child who participates in the Special Education program" is different than referring to a "SPED kid." This practice serves as a concrete reminder that a disability is but one characteristic of a child, and that a child is not defined by specific cognitive or physical limitations.

Another way to empower children with disabilities is to incorporate materials, such as books, in the classroom that feature characters who are disabled *and* possess many other distinguishing qualities. One teacher described her frustration with a lack of books featuring children with disabilities:

> Where are the books with characters who have disabilities and who engage with life in the rich and varied ways of more typically developing characters? Where is the book for my student who struggles to communicate her thoughts with her peers at school, much less join a sleepover? Or my student who struggles to play soccer with his classmates as he learns to control

his wheelchair? Or my student who has a meltdown whenever there is a minor change to our daily schedule?

(Pennell, Wollak, & Koppenhaver, 2017, p. 411)

Fortunately, the resources available to teachers and families continue to grow in response to shifts in beliefs and expectations about the role of school in the lives of children.

Asset Versus Deficit Perspectives

When teachers focus on what children *can* do rather than what they cannot yet achieve, they are demonstrating a fixed mindset, to use a term discussed in Chapter 4, but are also assuming that differences are greater than the similarities that create community. For example,

Figure 6.2 Dancer Collage

arrival, departure, and other transitions are important to all young children. Snack time and recess are times during the day when all children seek companionship and validation. The strategies that teachers might develop to address individuals' needs may differ, but these acts are no different than what any educator would do in any early childhood classroom where every child matters. Describing the behavior of a child on the autism spectrum, one parent shared the following sentiment:

> [Children] might prefer to sit quietly during lunch time. But they still want to sit next to other kids and feel their companionship. They just can't manage this task without the support of an adult.
>
> (McKenna, 2016, par. 9)

Teachers of young children can effectively develop and refine their practice to be sensitive to the diversity represented in a classroom community through pedagogy that respects children's individual and collective cultures in the broadest sense.

Expectations and Empowerment

In the late 20th century, intentional teaching practices that challenged the status quo in the interest of social justice and inclusion grew out of teacher-practitioner research. Two of the most influential pedagogical approaches are culturally responsive teaching and anti-bias education.

Culturally Responsive Teaching

The fundamental underpinning of *culturally responsive teaching* (Ladson-Billings, 1994) is a stance that acknowledges and celebrates precisely what makes every individual unique *and* how this stance, in turn, shapes children's thinking and learning. Characteristics of culturally responsive teaching include 1) a positive frame through which to engage with parents and families; 2) communicating high expectations for all learners; 3) student-centered instruction (e.g., building on children's interests and needs); 4) culturally mediated instruction (e.g., multiple and diverse perspectives and representations of information, material is relevant and appropriate); 5) reshaping the curriculum (i.e., to be interdisciplinary and meaningful); and 6) the teacher as facilitator, rather than holder and disseminator of knowledge.

In a culturally responsive classroom, teachers work with young children to extend and deepen their knowledge and enthusiasm. Children's language, values, and behaviors are respected and reflected in the classroom. In such an environment, motivation and culture are linked, which results in higher levels of engagement with curriculum, and, in turn, leads to higher academic and social-emotional outcomes for children.

Anti-Bias Education

Similarly, an anti-bias approach to education (Derman-Sparks & the A.B.C. Task Force, 1989) includes a philosophy and specific practices. The term *anti-bias*, often associated with educator Louise Derman-Sparks, is defined as

> an active, activist approach to challenging prejudice, stereo-typing, bias, and the "isms." In a society in which institutional structures create and maintain ["isms"], it is not sufficient to be non-biased (and also highly unlikely), nor is it sufficient to be an observer. It is necessary for each individual to actively inter-vene, to challenge and counter the personal and institutional behaviors that perpetuate oppression.
>
> (Derman-Sparks & the A.B.C. Task Force, 1989, p. 3)

More recently, educators have noted that anti-bias education "is inher-ently about change. This means embracing some level of uncertainty while holding tight to the vision of a more just world" (LeeKeenan & Nimmo, 2016, p. 66). Educators who are committed to anti-bias education recognize that being human means dealing with challenges presented in complex, evolving times. Anti-bias education provides teachers with a lens through which to view and interpret such chal-lenges—and the disequilibrium that often accompanies them—as learning opportunities instead of obstacles.

In a classroom that embraces anti-bias education, teachers rec-ognize that even if they never initiate conversations about "sensitive topics" such as race, gender, disability, death, religion, or many others, those issues are still present in the classroom because they are present in children's lives. "[W]e would be remiss to silence them in the school environment. Helping to provide language for our students to discuss these nuanced issues is a beneficial and incredibly important tool" (Jennings, 2015, p. 7).

Teachers strive to support children's development so that they are best able to persist in the face of obstacles and experience life's challenges as part of a system that cares about their well-being. Fortunately, society has responded to threats to students' well-being by establishing legislation that ensures protections inside and outside the classroom.

Legislation Designed to Protect and Assist Children and Families

There have been many significant laws passed over the last 100 years, and the sections below highlight some of the major milestones along the path to assuring an equitable, meaningful education for all young children. Drafting and passing such legislation is hard, often painful work. Over time, it becomes necessary to revisit legislation that may not provide equal, equitable education experiences for all citizens, and also to critically examine the boundaries between educational and social policies and practices. It is, however, the necessary effort to empower every child and family to achieve the ultimate educational objective—children's progress toward actualizing their fullest potential.

Plessy v. Ferguson

This decision by the U.S. Supreme Court in 1896 sanctioned the right of individual states to have "separate but equal" facilities for Black and White citizens. The federal government therefore permitted states to mandate racial segregation in public schools. Repercussions from this legislation continue to fuel debate and discussions at all levels (local, state, federal), as the current perceptions and lived experiences of children and families in different geographic locations in the United States reflect varying educational practices, despite legislative advances such as the decision below.

Brown v. Board of Education

In 1954, the U.S. Supreme Court unanimously agreed that racially segregated schools are "inherently unequal" and therefore the practice must be ended. As discussed in Chapter 5, critics of American public education today argue that public schools continue to be racially segregated, due to disproportionate access to resources in the environment, as well as state and federal funds that are tied to biased assessments and accountability measures. Two excellent books that address inequality in educational settings are *Savage Inequalities* (Kozol, 1991) and *Among*

Schoolchildren (Kidder, 1990). Though written several decades ago, the examples and lived experiences are as timely and relevant as ever.

McKinney-Vento Act

In 2000, President Bill Clinton renamed the (1987) federal legislation, which had previously been named after its major sponsor, Stewart B. McKinney, to include Bruce Vento's name as another one of the leading supporters of the legislation. The current legislation has been amended four times, each time strengthening the scope and conditions of the original law to provide emergency relief services (e.g., food and shelter), preventative measures (e.g., Medicaid), and long-term solutions to homelessness (e.g., efforts to increase affordable housing). Specifically, the amendments of 1990 specified in great detail the obligations of local and state entities in assuring children experiencing homelessness access to public education. Included in the amendments are specific requirements for states to provide funds that facilitate the implementation of this law.

Lau v. Nichols

This federal law, passed by the U.S. Supreme Court in 1974, mandates that children who have limited English speaking proficiency receive additional, "remedial" instruction to improve their English comprehension and speaking skills. While the 1974 decision did not provide specifics, it initiated further attempts to ensure that children have access to education that will help them thrive, as opposed to them being essentially excluded from meaningful classroom participation due to a language barrier. While the debate over whether bilingual education programs or sheltered English immersion programs are more appropriate for children's development continues, there are now mandated supports and curricula required in all public school classrooms. When state and federal funding is less than adequate, this mandate places significant financial burden on local districts that are required to provide necessary supports for children, and it raises questions about the federal government's commitment to education, particularly when mandates about standardized testing continue to exist and increase.

Title IX

This legislation applies to both public and independent institutions— any educational institutions that receive federal funding. Title IX is often associated with athletics, as that aspect has gained the most attention in the media, but the legislation applies to equality in terms of participation (equal opportunities to play, though identical teams may not exist for girls and boys); scholarships (equal/proportional dollar amounts for female and male athletes); equipment and supplies; access to tutoring and coaching; facilities and services; and recruitment. The law requires that policies, practices, facilities, and programs do not discriminate against *anyone* on the basis of gender—girls, boys, women, and men.

IDEA and IDEIA

In 1975 the Education for all Handicapped Children Act (Public Law 94–142) mandated that school-age children with disabilities would receive educational services, and in 1986 this law was extended (Public Law 99–457) to include preschool-age children through the Education of the Handicapped Act Amendments. At this time, legislators throughout the 50 states were urged to design and implement services for children from birth to age 3. Four years later, the original 1975 law was amended further, including a name change to the Individuals with Disabilities Act (IDEA). Replacing the term "handicapped children" with person-first terminology—"individuals with disabilities"—was an intentional attempt to shift assumptions and bias in a big way, through a relatively small change in language.

Subsequent amendments have been made since the IDEA amendments in 1990. For example, in 1991 legislation was passed (Public Law 102–119) requiring infants and toddlers to receive educational services in normalized settings, or natural environments. This means that young children with disabilities are to receive services in the home or formal educational setting where children without disabilities are—or would typically be—participating in educational activities. This translates into the requirement that consideration must first be given to placing children in a general education classroom, with appropriate support services, before they are removed and placed into a segregated classroom environment. The term for this approach is the *least restrictive environment*, and educators and administrators consider this to the greatest extent possible. Over the years, families and advocates for children have increasingly supported the idea that children have the right to experience the academic and social-emotional elements of education along with children of the same age or grade.

The IDEA legislation was most recently amended by Public Law 108–446, under what is now called Individuals with Disabilities Education Improvement Act (IDEIA). The most significant change is that under this law, young children can receive services without a more specific diagnosis than *developmentally delayed*. The expectation is that many children will receive effective early intervention services that may reduce later, delayed diagnoses.

In that same year, additional legislation was passed that had a big impact on children's education in schools and child care centers.

ADA

The Americans with Disabilities Act (ADA), amended in 2008, was designed to assure reasonable accommodations for all people with disabilities. The significant impact for early childhood education is that it ensures some fundamental rights for children with disabilities, specifically to access and accommodations in preschool and early childhood settings. This means that organizations cannot discriminate against children and their families based on disabilities and cannot exclude children unless their presence in the classroom presents a direct threat to the health and safety of others, or necessitates a fundamental alteration to the program.

Social reproduction theory (1970s)

> revolutionized the debate on the purposes and outcomes of schools and placed the success or failure of students in a new light. The benign, stated purpose of U.S. schooling to serve as an 'equalizer' is seriously questioned by these theories. For example, that the majority of students in urban schools drop out is not a *coincidence* but actually an *intended outcome* of the educational system. That is, according to reproduction theory, some students are intentionally channeled by the schools to be either fodder for war or a reserve uneducated labor force. Schools do exactly what is expected of them: They succeed at creating school failure.
>
> (Nieto, 2000, p. 235)

Educator and author Robert Lowe states, "Though long enshrined as a fundamental public good, public schools have been called on to serve contradictory aims: to engender critical citizenship and demand blind patriotism, to further group identity and promote group assimilation, to stimulate economic mobility and reproduce the class order, to enlarge equality of opportunity and maintain preserves of privilege" (as cited in Perry & Fraser, 1993, p. 271).

"There have been major gains for children in the last 25 years, but recent progress . . . has often not reached those children who need it most—because of geography, gender, ethnicity, disability, or because they are victims of conflict" (Geoghan, 2017, p. 1).

"There is no script for anti-bias work. We need to carefully analyze the situation from the child's perspective and context, respond appropriately in the short-term, and then develop deeper curricula responses and strategies based on the children's comments and the anti-bias goals" (LeeKeenan & Nimmo, 2016, p. 69).

Turning Ideas Into Action

Thumbprint

Goal: To develop awareness of similarities and differences among classmates

Materials needed: 3" x 5" index cards or small pieces of paper; ink pads of varying colors; pencils, pens; magnifying glasses; chart paper or other large writing surface to record children's ideas

Action: Present materials on a table. Invite students to make prints of their thumbs—thumbprints—explaining that they first press their thumb on one of the ink pads and then press their inked thumbs onto an index card, beginning with one thumbprint per card. Children may write their own names on the back of the cards displaying their thumbprints, or else teachers or classmates may do so to readily identify which cards feature which children's prints. Invite students to examine their fingerprints using the magnifying glasses. Ask the children, "How are these thumbprints similar? The same?" As children respond, encourage them to point out concrete places or ways that the thumbprints are the same. You may wish to record their ideas on a large piece of chart paper. After these answers have been shared, ask the children, "How are these thumbprints different? How are they not the same?" Again, invite students to point out specific details that support their thinking. Record these responses on a large piece of chart paper as well, either on a new sheet or adjacent to the first round of responses.

Extension: Once children have explored their individual prints, invite them to collaborate on team thumbprint pictures. Using their thumbprints as starting points, what shapes or images can they create? For example, a thumbprint can become the center of a sun, or the shell of a turtle, or the head of a lion, or the shield of a knight. The possibilities are endless, and several children can contribute their prints to a group thumbprint picture that they turn into a marvelous story.

Sensory Box

Goal: To develop awareness of what differently abled people can or cannot know based on sensory experience

Materials needed: Shoebox or other medium-sized box that has a hole cut in one side; several small objects that will fit into the box (e.g., toy car, seashell, doll, ball, metal key); scarf or bandana to cover children's eyes (optional)

Action: Place two or three items into the box and invite children to take turns feeling the items. For example, one child places her hand through the hole in the box and tries to identify the items by touch. If the child's eyes are closed or covered with a scarf/bandana, the child may remove the item from the box and try to use her sense of smell to identify the item as well. As the children explore the objects, ask them questions such as, "What do you notice about this item? What does it feel like? Is it rough? Smooth? Hard? Soft?" There are some questions that the child will be able to answer, and others that the child will likely not be able to answer, such as, "What color is it? What shape is it? What is it?" As children take turns, continue to ask them questions, encouraging them to notice what they could know from touching or smelling, compared with what they could know from seeing. They will likely share aspects of the activity that were hard and which were easier for them. Some children might share strategies that they used in identifying the objects, such as connections that they made with similar objects that they knew already.

Extension: To learn more about visual impairment, or other disabilities, see what tools and other equipment you can bring into the classroom for children to explore, such as Braille books or other items (e.g., Starbucks gift cards featuring Braille), eyeglasses with different prescription lenses, hearing aids, canes, and other equipment. The children may have ideas about equity and access that can be explored further. Examples of such advocacy efforts will be shared in Chapter 9.

The Light Inside

Goal: To help children understand the concept of "difference" through concrete noticing of physical, external differences, as well as the similarities that lie beneath the surface

Materials needed: Paper shapes (of different sizes, representing different textures, colors, and/or images) that may be glued together to create lamps; paper to glue upon; glue sticks or glue; flashlights

Action: Present materials on a table for children to explore and select. Talk with children about what they know about lamps. Where do they see lamps? What lamps do they see where they live? Invite children to select base pieces and lampshade pieces to glue on their paper to make a complete lamp. You may wish to have a model to show them. Tell the children that they may choose whatever pieces they would like to place together as they create their collection of lamps.

When the children have finished their lamps, discuss with them how each lamp is different—some lamps may be big, and some may be small. Some lamps may be crooked, and some may even be upside down! One thing that lamps share in common is light. Discuss with the children how no matter what lamps look like on the outside, they all have light that shines from the inside. While the lamp itself is the vessel, the light is what makes the lamp special. Explain to the children that the light inside of the lamp is similar to the personality or special something that we all have inside of us, and how that is something important to be valued and respected.

Extension: The song "This Little Light of Mine" is readily available for listening and viewing on YouTube, Spotify, and other online venues. Children can listen to and/or view performances of this song as they dance or move or enjoy choice/center time in the classroom. Discussion of differences and respect for all differences can extend to conversations about feelings, including how we feel when someone points out or laughs at our differences. This conversation can inform decisions about how and when to mention difference, and how this can be done respectfully, demonstrating empathy.

A Closer Look: Race, Gender, and Ability

Jason is a happy, healthy, intelligent 8-year-old boy. And he was born a girl.

When Jason was 5 years old, he told his parents, "Call me Jason. I'm a boy." His mother, Deena, felt uncomfortable with this request and talked with Jason's (born Samantha) preK teachers. The teachers explained to Deena that it is very common for children to want to explore the concepts of sex and gender and identity when they are young and defining the boundaries of their own understandings and of society's expectations.

The preK classroom featured gender-neutral toys, based on the teachers' beliefs that such toys allow as much flexibility in play as possible. The classroom also featured clothing that is typically attributed to one gender or another, such as skirts, dresses, and high-heeled shoes for girls/women and blazers, neckties, and loafers for boys/men. The teachers believed that children are starting to identify with specific gender traits at this time of their lives, and the clothing allowed children to "try on" different identities. During choice time, Jason chose the black waiter's jacket and red necktie. He often wore a hat to complete the look—a fedora or a boat captain's cap. The teachers had made note of this play and had not questioned it, since Jason seemed happy and played well with many classmates, creating fanciful, detailed stories to enact.

One Monday morning, Jason came to school with both of his parents, and when he went to color at one of the circle tables, Deena asked Sasha if she and her husband, Mikael, could speak with her. Sasha could tell that something important needed to be shared. "Deena looked like she was about to cry," Sasha would later relate. "Mikael looked like he had swallowed something really bitter. He had a really unpleasant look about him." Sasha asked the floater teacher to come into the preK classroom so that she could step out into the conference room with Deena and Mikael. The moment Sasha closed the door, Deena burst into tears.

"I am so scared, Deena!" she sobbed. "I am afraid we did a horrible thing." Deena began crying and was having a hard time speaking, so Mikael explained to Sasha that the family had been invited to a wedding, which happened two days prior. Deena had bought a "lovely dress" for Samantha, but Jason refused to wear it. They had spent over an hour trying to persuade him, cajole him, and bribe him into wearing the dress, but Jason simply refused to put it on, crying, kicking, and screaming, "I'm not a GIRL! I don't FEEL like a GIRL! I am a BOY! Let me live like a BOY!" over and over again.

"At one point, I was holding Samantha between my legs, kind of like a vice of sorts, and trying to force the dress over her head. After a few moments I looked up at Deena and I stopped cold. I just stopped cold. It just felt . . . cruel," Mikael said, swallowing hard.

"She's only five years old!" Deena cried. "How does she even know anything about anything like that?"

"I think you just know," Sasha said gently. "When it's causing this much distress, I think it's time to explore this a bit. We're all human beings, after all. What that means to one person may be different for another person, but don't you want Samantha to live her—or his—happiest life? We can help you."

***

"That was the moment something clicked in my head, and in my heart, really," said Deena, four years later. "I had to let go of the daughter that I had given birth to so that my son could live his fullest life. It was like mourning a great loss, which was really scary, but over time, and with a lot of support, we've all been doing really great."

Deena and Mikael joined a chapter of PFLAG—the national organization that supports parents of children who identify as LGBTQ—and began attending meetings regularly. They joined online discussion groups to learn about gender dysphoria, and about how they could support Jason, who began living as a boy at home and at school, and the whole family has been seeing a therapist together for family therapy sessions.

"At first I was so worried," Deena said. "I thought for sure the kids would tease him or pick on him, but they didn't! They were so accepting. It's as if they knew that he was a boy all along."

Jason registered for kindergarten at the local public school as "Jason—male." Deena and Mikael met with administrators and teachers to discuss how to support Jason's holistic health and well-being, and they worked through some initial bumps about which bathroom he would be allowed to use. Jason and his parents are now exploring hormone treatments that would simultaneously suppress his puberty trajectory to female and provide him with testosterone that would support his desired male development. Eventually, they will consult a physician about gender reassignment surgery, once Jason is old enough to undergo such procedures—likely when he is 18.

"We know that it won't always be easy," Mikael said, holding Deena's hand. "But we know it's the right thing for Jason. We feel validated every single day when Jason comes home from school and you ask him how his day went."

"Brilliant!" shouted Jason, raising a fist in the air and smiling.

Resources

Robert Coles on Ruby Bridges

https://video.search.yahoo.com/search/video;_ylt=A0LEVzArwo
Fa5MIA4xlXNyoA;_ylu=X3oDMTE0NTg2bDUxBGNvbG8DYmYxB
HBvcwMxBHZ0aWQDQjI5NDRfMQRzZWMDcGl2cw—?p=ruby+br

idges+robert+coles&fr2=piv-web&fr=aaplw#id=1&vid=48016bc7892c
9ae8339b79e0e7789761&action=view

This short video clip features Robert Coles discussing his relationship with Ruby Bridges and the insights he gained while they met and discussed her experience in the 1960s. This video provides an opportunity for students to see children's and adults' behavior, which contributes to racial tensions that exist today.

Kandice Sumner TED Talk

www.ted.com/talks/kandice_sumner_how_america_s_public_
schools_keep_kids_in_poverty

In this TED talk, Ms. Sumner shares her personal account of attending school out of her neighborhood district, and how her experiences and realizations of inequity shaped her current teaching practices back in her home neighborhood. The talk is provocative and raises issues about the historical roots of educational inequality/inequity in the U.S.

Rethinking Schools

www.rethinkingschools.org

This organization provides resources and literature developed for educators and families to address challenging topics that impact teaching and learning. Archives are searchable, and there are links to social media outlets that invite dialogue in the education community.

Note

1 "Life Doesn't Frighten Me" from AND STILL I RISE: A BOOK OF POEMS by Maya Angelou, copyright © 1978 by Maya Angelou. Used by permission of Random House, an imprint and division of Penguin Random House, LLC. All rights reserved.

References

Adichie, C.N. (2009). *The danger of a single story* [Video Speech]. Retrieved from www.ted.com/talks/chimamanda_adichie_the_ danger_of_a_single_story/transcript

BjohnsonEDU. (2018, February 26). *What we need to know about diversity in our schools via ASCD* [Twitter Post]. Retrieved from https:// twitter.com/bjohnsonEDU/status/968111453189361665

DeRosa, P., & Johnson, U. (2002). The 10Cs: A model of diversity awareness and social change. *The brown papers: Essays of reflection and analysis, 6*(5). Boston, MA: Women's Theological Center.

Derman-Sparks, L., & the A.B.C. Task Force. (1989). *Anti-bias curriculum: Tools for empowering young children*. Washington, DC: NAEYC.

Fine, C., & Elgar, M.A. (2017). Promiscuous men, chaste women and other gender myths. *Scientific American, 317*(3), 33–37.

Geoghan, T. (2017). *Stolen childhoods: End of childhood report 2017*. Fairfield, CT: Save the Children.

Green, J.F. (2018). They're not too young to talk about race! *Children's Community School*. Retrieved from www.childrenscommunity school.org/wp-content/uploads/2018/01/theyre-not-too-young. pdf

Hannah-Jones, N. (2016). Choosing a school for my daughter in a segregated city. *The New York Times Magazine*. Retrieved from www. nytimes.com/2016/06/12/magazine/choosing-a-school-for-my-daughter-in-a-segregated-city.html?mwrsm=Email

Jennings, A.J. (2015). 4-year-olds discuss love and marriage. *Rethinking Schools, 29*(4), 5–8. Retrieved from www.rethinkingschools.org/articles/4-year-olds-discuss-love-and-marriage

Kidder, T. (1990). *Among schoolchildren*. New York, NY: Harper Perennial.

Kozol, J. (1991). *Savage inequalities: Children in America's schools*. New York, NY: Random House.

Ladson-Billings, G. (1994). *The dreamkeepers*. San Francisco, CA: Jossey-Bass Publishing Co.

LeeKeenan, D., & Nimmo, J. (2016, November/December). Anti-bias education in challenging times. *Exchange*, 66–69.

McKenna, L. (2016). When kids sit alone. *The Atlantic*. Retrieved from www.theatlantic.com/education/archive/2016/09/when-kids-sit-alone/498587/?utm_source=eb

Nathan, L.F. (2017). *When grit isn't enough: A high school principal examines how poverty and inequality thwart the college-for-all promise*. Boston, MA: Beacon Press.

Nieto, S. (2000). *Affirming diversity: The sociopolitical context of multicultural education, 3/e*. New York, NY: Longman.

Olson, K.R. (2017). When sex and gender collide. *Scientific American, 317*(3), 44–49.

Pennell, A.E., Wollak, B., & Koppenhaver, D.A. (2017). Respectful representations of disability in picture books. *The Reading Teacher, 71*(4), 411–419.

Perry, T., & Fraser, J.W. (1993). *Freedom's plow: Teaching in the multicultural classroom*. New York, NY: Routledge.

Webb, S.L. (2018). I've never experienced white guilt. *Teaching Tolerance, 58*, 55–58.

7

Awareness of Self

Teachers of young children know that children enter the classroom with their whole selves, and this means that they bring with them visible traces of their home or other residential environment, as well as indications of their emotional states. They also bring with them invisible elements from these same sources—external and internal. The same can be said for teachers! Just as teachers strive to help children develop and move along the path toward their fullest potential, teachers also benefit from increasing their own self-awareness.

A teacher with a high level of self-awareness "recognizes that her lens completely shapes how she views her students and therefore her students' learning brains" (Rodriguez & Fitzpatrick, 2014, p. 124). Therefore the efforts involved in learning more about ourselves has direct benefits for the children with whom we teach and learn. In this chapter, information about mindfulness and contemplative practices is presented, as well as applications for classroom settings and further professional development. Activities at the end of the chapter reinforce the material and provide opportunities for teachers and children to open spaces for awareness, self-compassion, and respect for others.

Mindfulness

Because you are reading this book, you are already committed to strengthening children's grit, resilience, and motivation. The desire to achieve this goal is perhaps felt more intensely than before, due to the energy required to stay on top of the numerous tasks required of teachers—lessons to plan, before- and after-school responsibilities for self and family, pressures from administrators and/or families, as well as balancing your own activities and appointments. Mental and physical exhaustion is exceedingly common, and you may question your own stamina in a career about which you feel most passionate.

You are likely familiar with mindfulness. The concept of mindfulness is not new, yet in recent years practices that have existed for thousands of years have gained much attention and resonate with people of all ages, under the heading of *mindfulness*. Practices such as meditation and yoga have been examined through the mindfulness lens for the benefits that they bring to people's overall wellness, and these benefits have been backed up with scientific research. At its core, mindfulness is simply about paying attention. However, the intentional practice of paying attention is powerful because it brings about increased awareness of ourselves. This transformation

> comes directly out of our ability to take a larger perspective, to realize that we are bigger than who we think we are. It comes directly out of recognizing and inhabiting the full dimensionality of our being, of being who and what we actually are. It turns out that these innate internal resources—which we can discover for ourselves and draw upon—all rest on that awareness.
>
> (Kabat-Zinn, 2013, p. xxvii)

Dr. Jon Kabat-Zinn founded the Stress Reduction Clinic at the University of Massachusetts Medical Center and developed the Mindfulness-Based Stress Reduction program (MBSR). In his writing and speaking presentations, he explains the connections between our bodies and minds, as well as our mental practices and the scientific research that validates the experiences that many people live and grow with every day, over the course of our lifetimes. He explains:

> Mindfulness is a skill that can be developed through practice, just like any other skill. You could also think of it as a muscle. The muscle of mindfulness grows both stronger and more supple and flexible as you use it. And like a muscle, it grows best when working with a certain amount of resistance to challenge it and thereby help it become stronger.
>
> (Kabat-Zinn, 2013, p. xxxiii)

Mindfulness in education practices have grown across the country, including curriculum models that help integrate mindfulness into classrooms (see www.mindfulschools.org). For young children, understanding mindfulness as a concept may be more difficult than noticing the very real changes they feel in their bodies when they practice meditation. For example, in a children's book titled *Meditation Is an Open Sky* (Stewart, 2014), author Whitney Stewart writes:

> You know when you're having a bad day and
> nothing seems to go right? You have that WOBBLY
> feeling inside that makes you scared, sad,
> and mad all at the same time.
> Well, find a quiet place, sit down,
> and MEDITATE.
> Meditation won't take away your
> problems, but it will help you
> deal with them. You'll learn to
> watch your feelings pop up and
> disappear like soap bubbles.
>
> (pp. 6–8)

These words are significant because they describe for children how their feelings do not need to overwhelm them. It helps children understand that they are competent and capable of caring for themselves.

As children learn about and practice mindfulness, they experience the difference between simply knowing about feelings and knowing about their own feelings *in the moment*, as they are experienced. This is what Kabat-Zinn means when he emphasizes paying attention—bringing one's attention to the present moment to cultivate increased awareness. The ability to notice and identify feelings can therefore reduce the knee-jerk responses that we so often experience, and over time this contributes to a greater balance and sense of clarity in stressful moments.

Notice-Shift-Rewire

It is natural for us to want to avoid unpleasant, stressful feelings. But experts in mindfulness emphasize the important understanding that "when we use mindfulness to get rid of stress, we're no longer being mindful" (Langshur & Klemp, 2017, par. 10). They reiterate the fundamental element of noticing—allowing feelings and sensations to come and go. What this means is that in order to be mindful, we must nurture the mindful experience of stress, as opposed to trying to avoid stress in favor of more pleasant sensations. Authors Eric Langshur and Nate Klemp (2017) describe what they call the "Notice-Shift-Rewire" process, which helps people reframe and therefore experience stressful moments:

1. *Notice* the thoughts and physical sensations that go along with stress, including the moments when you find yourself enjoying the ease associated with avoiding the stress.
2. *Shift* your thinking to awareness without judgment, and try to simply notice what is happening in your body (e.g., tension in your shoulders, neck, or jaw; racing thoughts; increased heartbeat).
3. *Rewire* by sitting with the discomfort, rather than labeling it.

The authors suggest that following this simple sequence builds resilience. Children, for example, will come to recognize that stress isn't necessarily bad. By resisting or avoiding stress, we all lessen our ability to effectively cope with stressful situations. This argument is precisely in line with Kabat-Zinn's muscle analogy, in that the more practice children gain reimagining stressful moments, the more likely it is that they can use stress to their advantage. Similar with the idea of "growth mindset" discussed in Chapter 4, children can develop a "stress mindset" that empowers them rather than paralyzes them.

Loving Kindness

Another individual who is widely acknowledged as an expert in the field, specifically with regard to the notion of being kind and forgiving to ourselves as we are so often inclined to be toward others, is Sharon Salzberg. Salzberg emphasizes mindfulness as a choice. For example, most mornings we may wake up and go through our morning routine on autopilot. We can instead choose to wake up and notice the things that we often miss or ignore (Salzberg, 2011).

Through mindfulness practice, such as meditation, Salzberg (2013) suggests that we become more likely to embrace change and, ultimately, create change for ourselves. By creating a space for noticing our experiences in the moment, we become more adept at seeing the difference between what is actually happening and what we think and feel about what is happening. This is a critical distinction, and one that educators can work with children to practice. For example, in the moment, children may believe that a specific experience is permanent because it feels so big and so overwhelming—physically and emotionally. With time and perspective, children learn that feelings are temporary and kindness we direct toward ourselves provides us with courage to learn from these experiences and not be defined by them.

Some major principles of mindfulness may be summarized as follows:

◆ You are not your thoughts. While you cannot control *what* you think, you can learn to *notice how you respond* to what you think. This act of non-judgmental noticing breaks the cycle of thinking that often leads to worry and feelings of discomfort.

◆ Thoughts are fleeting, temporary ideas.

◆ Thoughts are influenced by a variety of factors, including heredity, past experiences, and the present moment.

Teachers of young children often incorporate elements of mindfulness or other contemplative practices without necessarily acknowledging them as such or being aware that they could be categorized this way.

Teaching as Contemplative Practice

Contemplative practices are those that invite reflection or introspection, such as meditation, as well as those that require focus and concentration, such as tai chi, painting, and hiking. When teachers incorporate contemplative practices into their teaching, they are cultivating an environment that supports compassion and empathy, reduces stress, and improves focus and communication skills for all members of the classroom.

For example, welcoming each student warmly each morning, or taking care—with intention and awareness—to send children back to their respective living environments at the end of the day, can occur while the teacher experiences the internal processes of *observation* (e.g., Natalia has some blotchy red dots on her face, neck, and ears), *registering "data"* (e.g., Josh didn't have his mittens this morning; this is the second snowy day he's been without snow gear), and *inquiry* (e.g., Will Alex assert himself when Rico takes the blocks from him this morning?). Each of these processes influences the other, much like a kaleidoscope when we turn it ever so slightly. It is interesting to notice how small adjustments to our teaching practices create new patterns and, in turn, impact children—and ourselves—in distinct ways.

The following sections describe small actions, anchored in mindfulness, that you can take in the classroom to strengthen your own contemplative muscle.

Pause

It is common for teachers to intervene when they see children struggling—to solve a problem or resolve a conflict. Many early childhood classrooms are often busy spaces filled with much energy. Sometimes this high energy is accompanied by high levels of noise. In a recent visit to a first-grade classroom during a science lesson, one child hypothesized that when tuning forks create vibrations, those vibrations need space. He stated assuredly that that was why the vibrating tuning fork caused a ping-pong ball to move upon contact. In a similar way, it is helpful to sometimes pause before rushing from one activity to another, or to interrupt a small group to provide them with information that they're missing or that would extend their learning into a new direction. By creating a small space between actions and interactions, you will be able to notice the difference that it makes. A simple way to create this space is to begin with a simple breath.

Breathe

One simple breath invites the opportunity for you to be present in your own body for that one moment. This strategy can be used when you choose to pause before acting (as noted above) or when you notice yourself feeling stressed or busier than is comfortable for you to be fully present in the moment or interaction. This technique is particularly helpful when children ask you many questions, such as at the beginning of the school year. If you want to establish a thinking routine that encourages them to check in with themselves first, or you suspect that they are capable of answering the questions themselves, this provides children with a moment to realize this or to decide upon strategies that may help them find the answers. Just as you may practice taking one breath before responding to children's questions, you can encourage children to take one breath before they ask questions. Over time, they will recognize that they know how to solve the problems or how to proceed to the next step in the process.

Notice

As mentioned earlier in the chapter, noticing what is going on in our bodies helps bring us back to the present moment when we feel out of control in any given situation. Creating a moment to do a quick check-in with our bodies can help us realize, for example, "I'm feeling really frustrated with the students right now. I'm so hungry—it's giving me a headache, actually." Such realizations—in a matter of seconds—help us realize that we are sometimes hijacked by our physical feelings and transfer those feelings into reactions to the people and situations around us.

Observe Without Judgment

Being able to notice what is happening without labeling what is occurring as good or bad, right or wrong, is particularly challenging for teachers. As educators, we are trained to design lessons with outcomes already in mind, and sometimes with assessments built into the lessons or experiences. The notion of evaluation is inextricably woven into the fabric of most lesson plans. The problem with this is that we are often so focused on what we think *should* happen or how we *should* teach that we miss children's own original ideas and opportunities to take learning in a completely different direction with much exciting potential.

In one of my favorite examples from classroom practice, an early childhood colleague, Mary, was feeling particularly tired one day while teaching an art lesson with 6-year-olds. The children were supposed to be rolling balls of clay, and one child in the group happened to be spinning around and around the pillar in one part of the room—holding the ball of clay in one hand and the pillar with the other. As he picked up speed, and Mary decided to ignore this behavior because she was too tired to redirect him, the ball of clay he was holding flew out of his hand . . .

. . . and because of the magic of physics and the composition of moist clay, this ball turned into a disc as it splatted onto the floor. Instead of scolding him and asking him to clean it up, Mary exclaimed, "Oooh! Look what happened!" Her curiosity blended with that of the rest of the children, who had numerous questions and hypotheses to explain the phenomenon. This launched an exploration that lasted several weeks. Noticing and following children's natural curiosity invites interest and engagement, rather than only concern about completing a lesson "successfully."

Beginner's Mind

Being able to sit comfortably with uncertainty is not easy for all teachers, or most people in general. The notion of a "beginner's mind" describes an approach or openness to thinking that includes unpredictability and diversity in terms of process and outcomes. There is also an element of humility involved with this type of thinking, in that we open ourselves to awareness of our own limitations and the fact that we do not know—or *need* to know—all of the answers to every question. Allowing yourself to participate in children's discovery as an able partner creates space for you to be available to children and honor their ideas.

Once children are able to identify how they are feeling and how those feelings influence their bodies and thinking, children—and teachers, too—benefit from the awareness of how their own feelings and senses of being influence the relationships and interactions they have with others.

The Impact of Self on Relationships

The quote below—one of my favorites—illustrates the need to feel and know connection between self and other:

> Piglet sidled up to Pooh from behind. "Pooh?" he whispered.
> "Yes, Piglet?"
> "Nothing," said Piglet, taking Pooh's hand. "I just wanted to be sure of you."
> (Milne, 1992, p. 120)

At any age, we often look to others to support ourselves, whether we are aware of seeking this support or not, and how we feel and act has an impact on those around us.

As young children begin to develop greater self-awareness, they will also discover the difference between their thoughts and the feelings and sensations that arise in connection with those thoughts. One can directly elicit the other. A child may think, for example, "I'm not good enough to score a goal for my soccer team," and the feelings that accompany that thought may include anxiety, anger, or sadness. The list below presents a variety of words to identify specific feelings, divided in categories, that can help initiate conversations with children with whom you teach and interact:

Angry—cranky, grumpy, irritable, seething
Happy—content, delighted, excited, optimistic
Sad—disappointed, gloomy, miserable, wretched
Scared—anxious, fearful, shocked, tense

Children will gain deeper understanding of these nuanced emotions by looking at photos or illustrations that clearly convey what certain feelings look like. There are wonderful examples of facial expressions that you can find online (see www.do2learn.com/activities/

SocialSkills/EmotionAndScenarioCards/EmotionAndScenarioCards. html) or in children's literature as well as nonfiction sources. You can co-create your own classroom "emotions chart" with students that provides concrete examples of feelings and what they look like on classroom members' faces/bodies. The conversations that emerge as children compare feelings words with images are rich opportunities to discuss how our individual perceptions and interpretations sometimes differ based on our own temperaments and experiences.

Researchers have made clear the explicit connections between emotions and social interactions:

> We all have emotions. And they consist of several elements. First, we usually have a conscious awareness of our emotions: when we are happy, we know it. Second, emotions typically affect our physical state: we show how we feel on our faces, in our voices, even in our posture; given the role emotions play in social networks, these physical manifestations are especially important.
> (Christakis & Fowler, 2009, p. 35)

Figure 7.1 Holding Ears

These authors further note that the development of emotions in humans over time, the visible display of emotions (as evident in Figure 7.1), and our ability to interpret the emotions of others played a fundamental role in the evolution of social activity in three specific ways: "facilitating interpersonal bonds, synchronizing behavior, and communicating information" (Christakis & Fowler, 2009, p. 36).

Some children find it the most natural thing in the world to share their thoughts and feelings through language, while others do not express themselves verbally and therefore teachers must learn to look for visual clues such as facial expressions, body language, and behavior. Providing children with opportunities to communicate through various means (e.g., words, pictures/books, actions) during the school day ultimately makes the work of the teacher that much simpler, taking some of the "detective work" out of the daily activity, leaving more time for observation and engagement with different focus areas.

Authentic and Effective Communication

One of the best ways to help children learn to communicate well through a variety of methods is to become better communicators ourselves. Teachers typically think that they must say or do the right things in order to be strong communicators, when one of the best techniques is to simply become a better listener. Notice your own behavior when a child is speaking with you:

Do you interrupt them while they are speaking?
Do you contradict their ideas or feelings because you want them to feel different or "better?"
Do you use physical expressions or gestures (e.g., eye-rolling, raised eyebrows, shaking your head) that contradict children's words?
Do you use physical expressions or gestures that validate their words (e.g., smiling, hands at rest, maintaining eye contact)?

Activating and embodying some mindfulness skills to be fully present with children sends a clear message to them that what they think and say matters, and therefore that they matter.

As teachers know well, sometimes communication is not verbal. Children communicate their wants and needs in many nonverbal ways, such as crying, maintaining close physical contact with someone or something, screaming, protesting, or seeking attention through some action. These methods of nonverbal communication occur differently for reasons related to children's abilities to communicate, the reasons for the communication, and the children's cognitive development and ability to understand social situations.

Your own goals for children's communication may or may not sync with the children's own goals in any given moment. Some strategies to help children develop communication skills include creating environments where language is seen and heard in many ways, such as 1) providing children with high-quality literature that is read aloud and independently; 2) incorporating art, music, and literacy activities that occur in small group and large group spaces; and 3) respecting language children bring into the classroom, including languages other than the dominant language spoken in the classroom, which is often English. The more that children know and feel that they are valued, the more open and accepting they tend to behave toward others.

Balancing Individual Needs and the Needs of Others

Researcher and author Tania Singer writes and speaks about "breaking the walls between people." As a German citizen, she remembers the moments in the late 1980s in which the literal walls between people came down between East and West Berlin, and she also recounts the breaking down of walls that existed in the minds of people at that time. It is in this vein that she discusses social neuroscience, specifically how our minds interact and communicate with other minds.

For the purposes of this chapter, Singer's discussion of the path from emotion contagion to empathy to compassion is relevant to how children's self-awareness impacts their relationships with others. To illustrate emotion contagion, she uses the example of how many babies begin crying when one baby starts to cry, or how children get the giggles because one child in a group starts snickering. Simply watching a video of infants or children behaving this way tends to induce similar emotions in adults, too (see www.youtube.com/watch?v=bUXZrKvT8JY).

Singer identifies the distinction between one person displaying an emotion and another individual sharing that emotion as our awareness of the difference between self and other. Once we recognize that we are distinct from others, we can observe and appreciate others' feelings (e.g., joy, pain), and we can literally feel these feelings through empathy. Singer argues that humans are hardwired to respond to the feelings of others in this way. She cautions, however, that it is important for us to recognize that the feelings of others are *not* our feelings. Singer believes this to be a very important distinction—moving from empathy to compassion—because while empathy allows us to share others' feelings, compassion moves us to care for others without embodying the emotional fatigue brought about by taking on others' feelings (Singer & Klimecki, 2014).

Because young children often have difficulty taking the perspective of others, not out of selfish, narcissistic tendencies but because their egocentrism is literally connected with their cognitive development (Böckler, Sharifi, Kanske, Dziobek, & Singer, 2017), it is helpful for teachers to provide opportunities for children to practice their observation skills and other social skills. As children develop more strategies for noticing and understanding others' feelings and perspectives, they are better able to communicate effectively and resolve conflicts.

Figure 7.2 presents one of many social media items shared by His Holiness the Dalai Lama of Tibet—with the explicit goal of motivating, inspiring, and helping others. In contrast with many people who use social media platforms to communicate—as is evident from a simple broad scan of posts and tweets—the 14th Dalai Lama chooses to use these platforms to reach a wide audience and encourage connections with others. In this example, the Dalai Lama's comment notes the absence of and need for compassion in contemporary education curriculum and contexts.

This explicit noticing and commentary underscores the desire of more educators to incorporate more social and emotional learning in classrooms, across all grade levels. The development of social-emotional learning (SEL) curriculum has followed a trajectory similar to the one that mindfulness curriculum has followed, and there are numerous agencies and organizations promoting an emphasis on critical skills for all school community members. The resources

 Dalai Lama ✔
@DalaiLama

 Following ⌄

Modern education pays little attention to inner values and yet our basic human nature is compassionate. We need to incorporate compassion and warm-heartedness into the modern education system to make it more holistic.

5:30 AM - 15 Jan 2018

Figure 7.2 Dalai Lama Tweet

at the end of this chapter provide some helpful material to extend your own learning.

As children develop empathy, compassion, and awareness of self in relation to others, it is important for them to understand that while they may care about others, they cannot control the thoughts and actions of others. For young children, who see the world through their own lenses and assume that everyone else does, too, having a concrete activity that helps them notice the difference between self and other helps build a solid foundation. Strategies can therefore be explored that increase compassion and protect children—and adults—from the fatigue that can accompany carrying others' concerns or discomfort. It is helpful for children to recognize the difference, and to literally identify where their own self ends and another person begins.

Therefore, becoming more aware of your own self and your own thinking helps you become a better teacher—one who can more effectively help children increase their own self-awareness. Children who are more able to create space for themselves when confronted with stressful situations will be better able to remain calm and respond to challenges, real and perceived. The efforts to increase self-awareness also have benefits in the form of healthy relationships with others. In the chapter that follows, we focus on the importance of relationships and responsibility for others.

Turning Ideas Into Action

My Majestic Mountain

Goal: To promote a sense of self-awareness and competence through visualization

Materials needed: A chair, cushion, or spot on the floor

Action: Invite children to find a comfortable position, either sitting on a chair or cushion or lying on the floor. Tell the children to let their hands rest in their laps or by their sides. The children may wish to close their eyes or gaze at a spot on the floor, or the ceiling if they are lying down. When the children are settled into their comfortable positions, read the following script to them. (Note: you can also record this in advance and participate alongside the children, or simply observe while the recording plays.)

Imagine you are looking at a big mountain—a majestic, beautiful mountain. This mountain may be one that you have seen or visited before, or it might be one that exists only in your imagination. Notice the mountain's shape—it may be pointy or bumpy. You might notice its sides, peaks, and the slope of the gigantic piece of earth. As you get closer to the mountain, you may notice trees growing on the mountain. Maybe there are animals grazing on it, and the sun may be shining above the top of the mountain. You may even notice snow decorating the higher peaks. Notice that the mountain is firmly planted in the earth. This mountain is still—it does not move; it is very strong.

As you continue to look at your mountain, notice that you have some things in common with this mountain. You are also firmly planted. You are also strong, and you are also beautiful. Imagine that your head is the top of the mountain and you can look around you and look at the land that surrounds you. Notice that your head is supported by the rest of your strong and sturdy body, and your shoulders and arms are the sides of the mountain, reaching down to your body's base—to your chair, or your cushion, or to your back resting on the floor.

Let's take a breath. With this breath, look at how the sun and clouds travel across the sky, making patterns and shadows that change, just as day turns into night. The stars and moon also move across the sky in patterns of their own. The light and shape of the moon changes from a sliver . . . to a half . . . to a full circle. Sometimes the moon is hidden behind the clouds. Each season brings changes to the mountain, too. In the summer there are bright green leaves on the trees, and grass growing on the surfaces of the slopes. In the fall the leaves change colors and drop to the ground. During the winter there is snow and ice on the top of the mountain and in spaces where the sun's warmth doesn't reach. And in spring, flowers bloom and leaves begin to grow on the trees. Listen to the birds' chirping across the peaks and valleys. What other animals do you see?

Extension: You may wish to simplify or adjust the visualization language or script. There are many meditations available online (see www.freemeditation.com/online-meditation/meditation-for-children/) and in books that are designed especially for young children (e.g., *Sitting Still Like a Frog, A Handful of Quiet*), based on their developmental levels and general characteristics of temperaments that often accompany childhood.

"I Am . . ." (or Being) Books

Goal: To increase self-awareness and promote self-forgiveness with concrete examples of everyday activity

Materials needed: Photographs of the children engaging in ordinary classroom activity and/or photos that family members send in of children engaging in activity outside of school; magazines; paper; glue sticks or glue; markers

Action: Write the following prompts on the pieces of paper that the children will use to create their "I am . . ." books:

- ◆ I am kind when _____
- ◆ I am gentle when _____
- ◆ I am curious when _____
- ◆ I am sad when _____
- ◆ I am scared when _____
- ◆ I am happy when _____

These examples are provided as a starting point, and you may wish to add others depending on the children's vocabulary and understanding of feelings and emotions. Invite children to finish the sentences, either writing their answers themselves or teachers doing so on their pages. When the children have completed the sentences, they can choose from images available to create an illustration for each sentence. They may wish to use a photo that depicts them in a specific activity, or else they can use a picture from a magazine, or draw their own.

When the children have completed their books' pages, these pages can be compiled into individual books that the children can read when they want to enjoy them, reminding themselves about the multiple dimensions that make up their complex selves.

Your Sleeve, My Sleeve

Goal: To introduce children to the concept of caring for others and identifying physical and emotional boundaries

Materials needed: Assorted long-sleeved clothing tops (e.g., shirt, sweater) of different fabrics/textures

Action: Invite children to sit together in pairs. Depending on the number of clothing items and the number of children who participate in this activity, you may wish to limit the pairs during a given activity time to maximize the opportunity for pairs to sit quietly and thoughtfully explore the clothing items' features. Ask the children to notice the sleeves of their own garments. What does the fabric look like? Feel like? Smell like? Is it smooth, bumpy, scratchy, slick, or other? Does it have a scent or particular odor? If so, what does it remind them of? Ask them to notice where their sleeves end. Unless the item is much bigger than their arms, the sleeves will likely end at the end of their own arms, their own individual bodies.

Now invite the children to feel their partner's sleeve. Ask similar questions as you did before. How is this sleeve different from their own sleeve? Point out to the children that while they may notice their partner's sleeve, it is not their own sleeve. They do not wear their partner's sleeve—that sleeve belongs to them. Helping children understand that their partner's sleeves aren't their sleeves is a tangible way for them to begin to understand that while they can appreciate something about another, they are not the other.

A Closer Look: Awareness of Self

Amelia stared down at her glittery flats as she walked down the hallway to her second-grade classroom. "Heel, toe, heel toe, heel, toe . . ." she repeated to herself as she carefully stepped inside one floor tile at a time, making her way past the kindergarten rooms and first-grade rooms. Amelia dreaded when Mr. Perez changed their table seats. She had her favorite spot—front table, to the right of the overhead projector. From this seat she could see the board, she could look out of the window to the playground, and she had an especially clear view of the daily schedule. She always liked to know what was coming next. So far, she'd been able to stay at the same table through two different seating shifts, and the last time she couldn't believe her luck! She hoped it would continue, but she was worried because on Friday Mr. Perez told the class that there would be some new seats for folks on Monday.

Amelia stepped into the room as Mr. Perez greeted students warmly, starting a phrase for the students to answer: "In the door . . . [dinosaur!]" "Here we go . . . [buffalo!]" "Find your seat . . . [parakeet!]" As he said the word "parakeet," Amelia felt her stomach lurch. She walked quickly over to her usual seat, and saw a new name plate taped onto the top of the desk: Tony. Tony! *TONY?!* He didn't even *care* about school anyway! Why did he get to have *her* seat? It wasn't fair. She felt like she was about to cry, so she turned toward the board and walked across to the next table . . . and the next . . . and then to the next row of tables.

She stopped in her tracks when she saw D.J., smiling and snapping his fingers, singing lines from a television commercial about "cars for kids." D.J. was always getting in trouble for talking. He was always goofing off, trying to get attention, but not in a good way. He had this funny laugh where he would giggle and then guffaw, and typically ended up with a fit of snorts or hiccups. Amelia couldn't believe that Mr. Perez would do this to her! She started to feel upset and could feel the sting of tears in her eyes. She turned back toward the front of the room, determined to tell Mr. Perez that she could not sit next to D.J., but then she thought that Mr. Perez must have had a very good reason for moving her seat next to D.J. Maybe he wanted her to help D.J. focus more, or listen more, or understand the reading more. That had to be it! She quickly wiped her eyes and turned back to her new seat, stashing her belongings in the shelf under her desktop.

"Helllooooooo, Ameeeeeliaaaaa!" sang D.J. as she sat down.

"It's time for the Pledge of Allegiance," Amelia said quietly, and she waited for the voice to come out of the speaker in the front of the room.

***

Over the next few weeks, Amelia tried hard to be a good role model for D.J. She helped him with their fractions worksheet, pointing out which answers he had to color in to make the picture turn out right. She let him use her pencil sharpener when his pencil broke—and it broke a lot! He chewed on his pencils, too, which she tried to ignore during quiet reading time. Amelia really wanted to do a good job so Mr. Perez would be proud of her.

One day, during social studies, Amelia and D.J. had to work together on a puzzle that was either a picture of pirates or pilgrims—she couldn't tell. Amelia always liked to finish the border of a puzzle first, so that she had a frame to work within, but D.J. kept grabbing a handful of pieces at a time, without even caring if they were edge pieces or not! She found herself getting frustrated, and then concerned. Time was almost up on the timer, and they hadn't even figured out what the picture was!

"Can you please stop just grabbing the pieces, D.J.? I can't tell what the picture is without the frame."

"It's Blackbeard. His real name wasn't Blackbeard, you know. It was Edward Teach," D.J. said, matter-of-factly. He tossed some puzzle pieces back and forth from one hand to the other.

"He was actually merciful, even if he did kill people as a pirate. He *always* offered mercy for people to surrender. If they didn't surrender, well, that's their *own* fault!" D.J. blurted, smiling. He tossed the pieces onto their desks and said, "Pick a piece, any piece, me hearty!"

Amelia chuckled, putting a hand over her mouth. She was actually surprised! How did D.J. know so much about pirates?

"How do you know so much about pirates?" she asked him, quietly.

"I know all about pirates! I used to love pirates more than football! I had my own pirate sword, and my own pirate hat—before my dog chomped it! Thar she blows!" he laughed and swatted his leg, leaning back in his chair, balancing precariously.

Amelia looked at Mr. Perez to see if he noticed that they were laughing, and she was relieved to see that he was grading worksheets at his desk. Maybe she was wrong about D.J. after all. She got back to work on the puzzle, thinking, "I have to focus. I have to help D.J."

***

One Friday, it was raining so hard outside that they didn't go out for morning recess, and at lunch they had to stay in the cafeteria, too. Everyone was feeling tired and a little antsy. Mr. Perez was reading to them while they sat on the rug—he hadn't done that in a long time. Amelia always loved read-alouds, even if they were kind of for babies. There was something really relaxing about sitting and listening to someone read you a story, especially if they could do funny voices for the different characters, like Mr. Perez.

"Amelia, look at this," D.J. whispered, and showed her a tiny ladybug that was in his hand. Amelia looked up at Mr. Perez quickly, then turned to D.J.'s hand, examining the ladybug. It was kind of yellowish more than reddish.

"They're good luck, you know," D.J. said earnestly, his eyes wide. "My dad told me so, so I try to protect them."

"Amelia, D.J.—listening ears, please," said Mr. Perez.

Amelia was mortified. She had caused Mr. Perez to interrupt his reading in front of the whole class! He'd never had to speak to her before about *anything*. And then she thought, "Oh, no! I forgot about being a good role model for D.J.!" She felt terrible, and full of shame. Her eyes stung, and she didn't hear a word Mr. Perez said after that, for the rest of the story time.

At the end of the day, as Mr. Perez was saying good-bye to the students ("See you later . . . [alligator!]"), she went up to him and looked down at her feet as she spoke.

"I'm sorry, Mr. Perez. I wasn't being a good listener. I'm sorry I wasn't a better role model for D.J." She choked on the last words as she spoke them.

"A role model for D.J.?" Mr. Perez asked, his eyebrows raised in surprise, and his hands on his hips.

"Didn't you move me next to D.J. so that I could help him and be a role model?" Amelia asked, looking up at him. Mr. Perez got down on one knee, and put one hand on Amelia's shoulder.

"I didn't move your seat next to D.J. for you to be a good role model," he said. "I moved your seat next to D.J. so that you would *loosen UP!*" He smiled. "Miss Amelia, you are one girl I never have to worry about. Remember that, ok? Just have some fun—school is supposed to include some *fun*, you know! How else could I be such an amazing teacher?"

***

Amelia always remembered that moment. As she grew older, she shared that story with friends and always smiled as she thought about how she had completely misread that situation. "We're all the stars of our own opera!"

Resources

What Do We Do All Day?
www.whatdowedoallday.com/childrens-books-about-being-different/

This website is dedicated to providing ideas and activities that will inspire children and families as they interact every day. This particular page is focused on self-esteem and "being different"—a feeling we all share at one time or another throughout our lives. The books and activities suggested provide a starting point for discussion with children of varying ages.

Child Mind Institute
https://childmind.org/article/the-power-of-mindfulness/

This organization strives to promote healthy development for all children and provides resources and insights to educators, families, and related care providers. There is much information related to mindfulness and stress reduction.

The Dalai Lama Center for Peace & Education: Educating the Heart
https://dalailamacenter.org/learn/videos

This web page provides links to numerous inspiring and motivating videos featuring prominent educators, psychologists, and others interested in teaching children to be aware, kind, and prepared to confront and cope with challenges they may encounter. The organization supports courses, conferences, and other related events that are noted on the website.

References

Böckler, A., Sharifi, M., Kanske, P., Dziobek, I., & Singer, T. (2017). Social decision making in narcissism: Reduced generosity and increased retaliation are driven by alterations in perspective-taking and anger. *Personality and Individual Differences, 104*, 1–7.

Christakis, N.A., & Fowler, J.H. (2009). *Connected: How your friends' friends' friends affect everything you feel, think, and do.* New York, NY: Back Bay Books.

Dalailama. (2018, January 15). *Modern education pays little attention to inner values and yet our basic nature is compassionate. We need to incorporate compassion and warmheartedness into the modern education system to make it more holistic* [Twitter Post]. Retrieved from https://twitter.com/DalaiLama/status/952850556330033152

Kabat-Zinn, J. (2013). *Full catastrophe living: Using the wisdom of your body and mind to face stress, pain, and illness.* New York, NY: Bantam Books.

Langshur, E., & Klemp, N. (2017). Being with stressful moments rather than avoiding them. *Mindful.* Retrieved from www.mindful.org/being-with-stressful-moments/

Milne, A.A. (1992). *The house at Pooh Corner.* New York, NY: Puffin Books.

Rodriguez, V., & Fitzpatrick, M. (2014). *The teaching brain: An evolutionary trait at the heart of education.* New York, NY: The New Press.

Salzberg, S. (2011). *Real happiness: The power of meditation: A 28-day program.* New York, NY: Workman Publishing.

Salzberg, S. (2013). *Real happiness at work.* New York, NY: Workman Publishing.

Singer, T., & Klimecki, O.M. (2014). Primer: Empathy and compassion. *Current Biology, 24*(18), R875–R878.

Stewart, W. (2014). *Meditation is an open sky: Mindfulness for kids.* Park Ridge, IL: Albert Whitman & Company.

8

Responsibility for Others

The children's book *Swimmy* by Leo Lionni (1963) illustrates the fluid and interdependent nature of being oneself and being in relation to others. The protagonist, Swimmy, teaches his friends how to escape danger by working together, and he recognizes his own critical role in the process. Young children are born with specific needs that require the help of others, and they are unable to understand or take the perspective of others for several years. Yet human nature is wired to seek out social interaction for more than basic needs. One of the wonderful aspects of being human is that we continually evolve and change. Each day brings experiences and events that impact our lives, with potential to help repair cognitive, physical, or emotional damage. Since young children often adapt readily and with less difficulty than adults, the early childhood years are particularly special, and a time when relationships with others are essential to establish and nurture.

In Chapter 7, the concept of loving kindness was presented in the context of mindfulness and self-awareness—being kind to ourselves and recognizing our strengths is a critical part of healthy development. In this chapter, we shift the lens outward to consider how relationships with and responsibility for others impact children's grit, resilience, and motivation. "Both science and wisdom traditions promise that the more we share—be it stuff, protection, or wisdom—the more we receive in return. What we give is less important than the intention behind the act of giving. Generosity opens our heart and connects us with others. In this way, it helps dissolve the divisions between self and other and radiates loving kindness out into widening circles" (Willard, 2017, p. 25).

Early childhood teachers know that the concept of sharing—of taking something that is yours and *giving* it to another—is not always easy for young children to do, or to understand as a positive act. I often remember the words of a dear family friend—a child psychiatrist—who says that for a young child, "to share is to *lose*." As children develop awareness, empathy, and compassion, they demonstrate their consideration of others more readily (as visible in Figure 8.1), but it is also important to honor the qualities and capabilities that children bring with them. Grown-ups sometimes underestimate the instincts that children possess.

Figure 8.1 James Feeding Bear

"It's hugely important never to forget that the theories we form of students are in fact *theories*, not truths. Often we act upon them as if they are facts, leading to a dangerous rigidity in our understanding of ourselves and our students" (Rodriguez & Fitzpatrick, 2014, p. 124). The sections that follow present some challenges to children's successful relationships with others, and information that teachers can use to collaborate with children, families, and the broader community to sustain an environment where children feel connected and safe, and excited to learn.

Relationships, Responsibility, and Resilience

As noted above, children are born wired for social interactions. On a purely evolutionary level, "in human existence it became essential for humans to rely on one another for safety and security in order to thrive in an environment of constant threat" (Langworthy, 2015, p. 9). The relationships that children established and benefited from at birth were vital for survival. While we no longer need to worry about saber-tooth tigers surprising us at our doorsteps, there are very real threats that young children perceive and come to know in their respective environments.

Throughout this book, relationships have been touted as fundamental to children's resilience. It is also important to consider how relationships may sometimes threaten children's successful development, and how teachers may act to interrupt the negative patterns that form and set a course for a healthier trajectory.

Trauma

The word *trauma* is currently used quite often in educational parlance, as teachers have begun to recognize patterns in children's behavior that stand out from "typical" child development. Most teachers do not receive explicit coursework in their teacher preparation programs that focuses on trauma—how to recognize signs of trauma and strategies for helping children who have experienced event-specific or long-term (i.e., chronic) trauma. What they may experience in the classroom is a child whose behavior is having a detrimental effect on their social relationships and academic success. Whether or not teachers know or later learn facts about traumatic events (biological and/or environmental) that were related to a particular child, teachers can learn some fundamental information that helps them become active advocates for children. The first step is an understanding of just what trauma is and what it is not.

People tend to think of violence, such as severe neglect or abusive experiences and relationships, when they hear the word *trauma*. This is not necessarily accurate. For example, children may experience trauma in utero—due to a mother who is experiencing her own stress and the resulting physiological effects on her own body and, therefore, that of her developing fetus. For a young child in distress, her brain and body prioritize survival over social interactions in an unconscious, instinctual response. Though the child is unaware of this, her body is responding with laser-sharp focus on the question, "Am I safe?" (Desautels, 2016, par. 4). There are some specific elements related to trauma that are important to distinguish and understand effectively so as to best address the needs of children in the classroom.

Stress and Response

In Chapter 2, the fight-or-flight stress response was presented in connection with children's ability to respond and persist in the face of adversity. As a brief recap, when humans experience stress, the body kicks into gear and releases several hormones, including adrenaline and cortisol. These hormones are crucial because they help the human body and brain cope with potentially threatening situations, real or imagined. Adrenaline is responsible for increases in heart rate, our heightened attention or vigilance, and blood flow to muscles and different parts of the body. Cortisol helps the body fortify itself in order to best handle the situation and maintain a state of consistent alert and efficiency. Cortisol is ultimately responsible for priming the body to fight or flee from a threat. When children experience trauma, the stress response is activated. When children experience trauma and the stress response over a prolonged period of time, the impact on their development can be significant, though relationships with caring others have been shown to be the "active ingredient" in human development (National Scientific Council on the Developing Child, 2004). There are three categories of stress to consider in children's development: positive stress, tolerable stress, and toxic stress (Langworthy, 2015).

Positive stress is the most common type of stress that we all experience. It involves minor, short-term occurrences that are manageable and temporary. For example, a child might feel an increase in her heart rate before participating in a preschool sing-along, or a rush of adrenaline before the word "GO!" that launches a race during recess. While children experience the physiological effects of stress in these instances, they typically dissipate once the event is over, and the stress often serves to boost their performance rather than hinder it.

Figure 8.2 Toddler 2 Car Race

Tolerable stress includes experiences that are more intense than those associated with positive stress and that can be detrimental to children's cognitive and social-emotional development. Examples of tolerable stress include the death of a family pet or loss of personal possessions due to a house fire or burglary. These experiences absolutely create challenges for children emotionally and sometimes include physical responses (e.g., irritability, sleeplessness, fatigue, stomachaches) along with the hormonal reactions connected to the body's stress response, but these responses are time-restricted because children tend to recover and rebound with the support of caring individuals and social networks in their lives.

Toxic stress presents the most challenges to children's development, due to the long-term and intense quality of the stress or trauma. Situations such as chronic homelessness, abuse from a caregiver, or extreme poverty elicit the body's stress response for prolonged periods of time, at higher frequency. Over time, the body tends to adapt to this heightened state as the "normal" state, one with which other systems must function (Langworthy, 2015). This can have a lasting impact on children's brain development and behavior. "Children who experience toxic stress tend to be more hypervigilant, as if expecting or anticipating threatening situations" (p. 41) as a routine part of their daily lives.

Consistent with the findings of researchers Werner and Smith, discussed in Chapters 1 and 3, research focused on toxic stress has suggested that interactions with caring, responsive caregivers play a critical role in reducing the negative effects that toxic stress has on brain development, function, and children's behavior. A child's confidence in the consistent presence and support of a caring, responsive caregiver disrupts children's biological responses to stressful experiences, in addition to their behavioral reactions (Langworthy, 2015). From a teacher's perspective, a child's brain may be affected by exhaustion, hunger, worry, or neglect, and what the teacher sees is the child's expressing of the associated feelings of fear, isolation, frustration, or anger. Teaching can be most effective when "the act of successful teaching occurs in a large, encompassing system, in which the teaching brain and the learning brain are dynamically interacting" and:

1. The teacher senses student-centered information.
2. The teacher **processes** the information he or she has pulled in that is relevant to how the student learns.
3. The teacher then utilizes this processed information to **respond**, offering the student support to improve the depth of his or her learning.

(Rodriguez & Fitzpatrick, 2014, p. 83)

How can teachers best create and sustain calm and safe brain states for themselves and for the children with whom we teach and learn? The first step is to establish an environment that supports the physical and emotional safety of all who enter the space. In such a learning environment, teachers shift their focus from trying to change or stop challenging behaviors to understanding why children are behaving a certain way. When teachers recognize the signs of trauma, and understand the effects of trauma on the brain, they can better understand the triggers for certain emotional or behavioral reactions.

Some professionals have frameworks or strategies for working with children who express challenging behaviors that stem from traumatic experiences. These patterns can cause behaviors that seem hostile but are actually unconscious attempts to protect themselves. Teachers can help children learn to change these patterns. They can help children recognize when their bodies feel highly aroused, and calming the nervous system is one of the simplest ways to bring the body to a more regulated state. Practicing deep breathing, meditation, or visualization—even for less than five minutes—has a measurable impact on children's nervous systems and provides them with concrete evidence that they can control this aspect of their bodies.

Although it seems contradictory, sometimes movement is equally helpful to calm the nervous system and relieve stress on the amygdala. Children can use movement activities, such as dance, yoga, jumping jacks, or other actions, to calm their brains and help bring their focus back to learning. As children experience different options to move their bodies, they are empowered to recognize their physical state of being and make decisions about when they might need to take a walk, stretch, or even run outside for a while.

The value of movement in the daily classroom activities that young children experience is particularly high in classrooms that incorporate more academic desk work and worksheets than open-ended learning activities in which children move about the room. It is not uncommon for some children to spend an hour at a time sitting and filling in paper-and-pencil worksheets, often in preparation for standardized assessments that they are being prepared to take, sometimes as young as 5 years old. It is interesting and ironic to examine the impact of technology on children's relationships and development in this light, since one of the main arguments against the use of technology in early childhood classrooms is that it inspires too much sedentary activity.

The Impact of Technology on Children and Families

Many teachers of young children are faced with the challenge of explaining the use of technology in early childhood classrooms, in part because parents and others assume that the use of digital tools will make children—to be blunt—lazy, fat, and antisocial. As discussed in earlier chapters, discomfort with something different or unfamiliar is not a new phenomenon, and in this case, adults' discomfort with new and emerging technology tools is no different. It is astounding how quickly young children—even toddlers!—can pick up a tablet or smartphone and swipe instinctively, or otherwise access features about which the adult owners of the devices are uncertain. Examples such as this illustrate how growing up with such technology as a part of their daily environment has led to the term "digital natives" (Prensky, 2001) being used to describe the generations of children who have been born with access to these tools. Furthermore, interacting with a diverse array of digital tools has become a natural part of children's play. In recent years, researchers have examined how children's access to technology influences children's social relationships and development (Hutchby, 2001).

Technology

One of the most prominent researchers in the field of technology and human interaction is Sherry Turkle, a professor and the founder and director of the Initiative on Technology and Self at the Massachusetts Institute of Technology. Much of Turkle's oft-cited research responds to the perceived detrimental influences that technology has on interpersonal relationships. For example, Turkle cites one classroom discussion with students in which they "don't feel they can be present unless they are also, in a way, absent" (Turkle, 2015, p. 212) because they are compelled to text and check text messages during her class.

Turkle also explains that the use of various devices causes people to pay a price in their capacity for solitude, and she sees an important connection between the capacity for solitude and the capacity for conversation. Turkle cautions that adults may need to reteach the value of solitude to children, but this is challenging because adults have lost sight of the value, too. For example, Turkle explains:

> The mere presence of a phone on the table (even a phone turned off) changes what people talk about. . . . And conversations with phones on the landscape block empathic connection. If two people are speaking and there is a phone on a nearby desk, each feels less connected to the other than when there is no phone present. *Even a silent phone disconnects us.*
>
> (Turkle, 2015, p. 21)

When we consider the impact of such disconnect on people across different generations, such as parent-child or teacher-child, these communication and empathy challenges can contribute to what Turkle calls "disconnection anxiety." Turkle argues that it is precisely this anxiety that leads people back to their devices. Children, like all humans, want to know that people care about them.

Social Media

As teachers and caregivers attempt to navigate the ever-changing, fast-paced world that includes the Internet and the cloud, it is sometimes dizzying to keep up with the social media sites and jargon that accompanies participation in these outlets.

Any Web site that allows social interaction is considered a social media site, including social networking sites such as Facebook, MySpace, and Twitter; gaming sites and virtual worlds such as Club Penguin, Second Life, and the Sims; video sites such as YouTube; and blogs. Such sites offer today's youth a portal for entertainment and communication and have grown exponentially in recent years.

(O'Keeffe & Clarke-Pearson, 2011, par. 1)

Rather than struggle against the digital current that sometimes feels, to teachers and parents, as powerful as a riptide that can carry children out into the digital ocean if they don't pay attention, it is helpful to understand that children's online lives are, in fact, an extension of their offline lives (O'Keeffe & Clarke-Pearson, 2011).

Taking an active and engaged stance in this digital world is, therefore, similar to being present in children's other social activities. For older children, risks associated with social media include cyberbullying and harassment, sexting, Facebook depression, privacy concerns, leaving a digital "footprint," and the influence of advertisements on buying decisions. A digital footprint refers to traces of evidence that people leave behind when they post or respond to social media. It is important for children to understand "netiquette" early on, for the simple reason that these traces can be found years later. A child doesn't necessary think about how what she posts online might appear years later when a potential employer decides to examine her Twitter or Facebook history. Similarly, children do not often consider how businesses target or identify people based on their web-browsing behavior. It is sometimes unsettling to notice how ads tend to appear that are somehow related to something searched for days ago, so it is important to teach children to recognize these subtle connections:

Many online venues are now prohibiting ads on sites where children and adolescents are participating. It is important to educate parents, children, and adolescents about this practice so that children can develop into media-literate consumers and understand how advertisements can easily manipulate them.

(par. 15)

There are laws in place to protect children's privacy, but not all teachers and caregivers are aware of them. For example, 13 years of age is the minimum age for most social media sites because 1) 13 years is the age established by Congress in the Children's Online Privacy Protection

Act (COPPA), which forbids websites from gathering information about children younger than 13 years without parental consent; and 2) official terms of service for many sites now set 13 years of age as the minimum age to sign up and create a profile. However, there are many sites for younger children that do not have such age restrictions, so it is important for teachers and families to be conscientious about the software and Internet sites that they utilize in the classroom and home environments.

Shifting Roles

It has become quite common for children to know more than adults about the online tools and sites that they use and visit. For some adults, this causes them to experience disequilibrium:

> In children's interactions with parents and other adult authority figures, one obvious effect has been the frequent reversal of the traditional parent-child relationship with the computer-savvy child taking on the role of teacher to the parent. . . . In addition, some have hypothesized that the equality in online communications among computer users of all ages tends to erode authority structures.
>
> (Subrahmanyam, Kraut, Greenfield, & Gross, 2000, p. 131)

As digital technologies become a consistent presence in the classroom and home environments, adults are becoming more comfortable with the tools as well as with what they do not know.

It was also the case several years ago that there was a perceived gender discrepancy in terms of who chose to access computers and the Internet and who did not. One study found that boys spend more than twice as much time per week playing computer games and are five times more likely to own a computer system. The researchers also state that "boys tend to prefer pretend play based on fantasy, whereas girls tend to prefer play based on reality—a rare theme for computer games, even those designed specifically for girls" (Subrahmanyam, Kraut, Greenfield, & Gross, 2000, p. 131). Over the last decade, computer games have evolved to appeal to a wide audience, and the familiarity with specific tools has decreased the perceived gender gap in access to and interest in computers and the Internet. Researchers continue to examine the role of computers and the Internet in classroom environments. Though they "are widely used by children for schoolwork and to obtain information, more and better evidence is needed to support the claim that home computer use can improve school performance" (p. 139).

As the premier professional organization of educators in the United States, the National Association of Educators of Young Children (NAEYC) includes in its Position Statement (2011) the following core values, among others (see www.naeyc.org/sites/default/files/globally-shared/downloads/PDFs/resources/position-statements/Ethics%20Position%20Statement2011_09202013update.pdf):

◆ Appreciate and support the bond between the child and family
◆ Recognize that children and adults achieve their full potential in the context of relationships that are based on trust and respect

Ethics and empathy may be modeled and taught through digital means, but when early childhood educators keep such values at the heart of the work they do with children and families, personal relationships remain the cornerstone of children's classroom experiences and resonate throughout children's development.

Ethics and Empathy

Consideration for the well-being of others is a fundamental part of everyone's existence. Teachers can help children develop their skills so that they may make ethical decisions. "By thinking, speaking, and acting skillfully today, we and our children will be more likely to think, speak, and act skillfully tomorrow—it's that simple" (Willard, 2017, p. 50). The ordinary, daily interactions between children and those who care for them contribute to a biological foundation that children carry with them—unconsciously and consciously—throughout their lifetimes. In Chapter 4, author Andrew Newberg recalled some important lessons he learned from being convinced to eat his peas as a child. These lessons had a lasting effect:

Today, I continue to treat the world as an interconnected whole, where everyone and everything has value and a place and is to be treated with equal kindness and respect. And it all began with a series of childhood beliefs: the belief that you have to listen to your parents (at least some of the time); the belief that vegetables are good for you (at least some of the time); and the belief—which was triggered by an overwhelming feeling of guilt—that peas had feelings and friends.

(Newberg & Waldman, 2006, p. 104)

There are long-term benefits of empathy and compassion that impact our own well-being and that of others. "Each generous action we take rewires the brain for happiness and resilience, one good deed at a time" (Willard, 2017, p. 11). As children enter into relationships with people around them, they learn about differences and similarities, which may include ethnicity, racial identity, economic level, family structure, language, and religious and political beliefs. All of these cultural elements profoundly influence children's development and their relationships with each other and with the world.

Historical Milestones in Social Welfare and Child Welfare Reform in the U.S.

As noted throughout this chapter, one of the most widely acknowledged goals in the United States, and throughout the global community, is a commitment to the overall well-being of all citizens. Social welfare programs were designed in the U.S. to support the standard of living, health, and education of citizens. From a historical perspective, there have been many significant programs established and modified throughout the course of this country's development. The events mentioned here are notable, but there are many other events that have contributed to the current social welfare programming in the U.S. Over time, changes in economics (e.g., rural vs. urban concentration; agricultural vs. technological production) and population growth, for example, have impacted some of the major milestones along the path to assuring equitable, accessible care for all citizens, from birth to death.

As emphasized in Chapter 6, it is important and necessary over time to revisit legislation and programming and to critically examine social policies and practices. As you read the information in this section, consider how social welfare programs in the U.S. help (or hinder) every child and family to achieve and sustain fundamental well-being.

Turn of the 20th Century—Policies and Practices

Throughout the first part of the 20th century, several different programs were initiated that continue to this day. These initial efforts set the course for later design and expansion, and they acted to sustain a rapidly evolving citizenry during the First World War and the Great Depression. For example, in 1906 the **Federated Boys' Club** was formed, which is now known as the Boys & Girls Clubs of America. In that same year, **the Pure Food and Drugs Act** was passed, which required the federal government to oversee the safety and quality of foods and medicines. These responsibilities are now upheld by the Food and Drug Administration.

In 1907, the first **Federal Employment Service** was created to help match workers with employers, and this service is now continued in the U.S. Employment Service. Two years later, in 1909, the **National Association for the Advancement of Colored People (NAACP)** was formed by Black and White citizens committed to social justice.

In 1912, the state of Massachusetts authorized the first **minimum wage law** in the country, and the **Children's Bureau** was established to protect the health of mothers and children. In 1920, the **Child Welfare League of America** and the **U.S. Veterans Bureau** were founded. In that same year, the **19th Amendment** to the U.S. Constitution guaranteed women the right to vote.

1930s—Planning With Purpose

As the country struggled to recover after the Great Depression, President Franklin Delano Roosevelt (FDR) mobilized the federal government to provide relief and aid to its citizenry. Historians attribute FDR's commitment to the well-being and welfare of all members of society to the influence of and inspiration provided by his cousin, Theodore Roosevelt, and FDR's wife, Eleanor Roosevelt.

In 1935, the **Social Security Act** was passed to support the needs of America's most vulnerable citizens: children, the elderly, and families whose financial stability was in jeopardy. Prior to this, the needs of vulnerable populations were addressed by local "settlement houses" (establishments, often in urban settings, that provided basic services to community members), which evolved from our country's original practices of family bearing responsibility for dependents, with the mutual assistance of neighbors and friends as secondary support, when available. This act provided assistance with unemployment, maternal and child welfare, and social security.

After World War II, President Roosevelt attempted to increase programming to include benefits that would increase citizens' access to food, housing, and recreation, a living wage, and adequate medical care. Unfortunately, he died before many of these efforts were realized. He did, however, sign the **Fair Labor Standards Act** in 1938, which 1) formalized the minimum wage; 2) required overtime pay for employees and accurate recordkeeping by employers; and 3) established youth employment standards in the private and government sectors.

1960s—Expansion and Evolution

During this period, services and programming for American citizens expanded to include some very significant amendments. Two critical acts that greatly impacted the populations often served by social welfare programs included the **Civil Rights Act** of 1964 and the **Voting Rights Act** of 1965. The legislation known as the Civil Rights Act was passed to eliminate discrimination based on race, color, religion, sex, or nation of origin, and impacted voting, education, accommodation, and employment practices. This act is considered to be one of the hallmarks of the Civil Rights Movement. In the subsequent year, the **Voting Rights Act** was signed into law by President Lyndon Johnson. It enforced the 15th Amendment to the Constitution and outlawed obstacles to voting that had prevented African Americans and others from even registering to vote, thereby severely limiting their political power.

Also in 1965, **Medicare** (Title 18—medical care to all over 65 years of age) and **Medicaid** (Title 19—medical care for poor family members of any age) were established, increasing the proactive measures that could improve people's lives and livelihoods. Other significant actions in this proactive vein included the establishment of the federal **Department of Housing and Urban Development**, the passing of the **Food Stamps Act**, and the passing of the **Housing and Urban Development Act**. All of these helped pave the way for the **Supplementary Nutrition Assistance Program (SNAP)**, which is—at the time of this writing—one of numerous programs whose funding is in jeopardy. According to the Children's Defense Fund (see www.childrensdefense.org/library/data/child-poverty-in-america-2016.pdf), SNAP helped raise 1.5 million children out of poverty in 2016. This pattern of cuts to social welfare programs was evident in the decades following the 1960s, and particularly in the 1980s, which led to another wave of change in the final decade of the 20th century.

1990s—Change and Reform

In 1990, the **Americans with Disabilities Act** was signed into law by President George Bush. The legislation prohibited discrimination in hiring and in the workplace against people with disabilities. It also outlawed discrimination in public activities, public transportation, public accommodations (e.g., theaters, hotels, restaurants), and telecommunication systems (i.e., for people with speech and/or hearing impairments). Several years later, in 1997, the **Children's Health Insurance Program (CHIP)** was expanded, and like SNAP, this program is threatened by currently proposed federal budget cuts. Termination of this program will impact access to health care for up to 9 million children in the U.S.

Future Directions

One of the most controversial acts to have been passed in recent years is the **Affordable Care Act (ACA)** that President Barack Obama signed into law in 2010, after several years of difficult political and economic negotiations. When he entered his presidency, President Obama was, like President Franklin Delano Roosevelt, guiding the U.S. out of financial trouble. The health-care reform was seen as an opportunity to significantly expand access to quality health care for the first time since the origins of Medicare and Medicaid. There remain numerous needs for children, families, the elderly, and individuals who are disabled or live at or below the poverty line. What is the role of teachers? Teachers, by virtue of their profession, are responsible for others every day, and this responsibility often extends beyond curriculum into other domains as teachers work and grow with children and families.

Perhaps one of the most important actions that educators can do—in the short term—in order to effect meaningful change is to vote in elections every year. In the long term, teachers can encourage children to become active in civic engagement, and teachers can also model this behavior in and out of the classroom, advocating for human rights and effective social welfare programs. The topics of activism and engagement will be discussed more fully in the final chapter, along with activities and resources to reinforce these concepts.

Turning Ideas Into Action

Perspective Painting

Goal: To encourage children to pay attention to the actions of others, thereby interpreting and coordinating their own actions with those of another

Materials needed: Tempera paints of various colors; paintbrushes; a clear sheet of plastic (approximately 16" x 24") or a window that children can paint on from opposite sides, facing each other. (Note: You may find a window outside someone's house on trash collection/recycling days, or perhaps a family at the school is replacing windows in their home and can donate one to the classroom. Otherwise, children can take turns painting on opposite sides of a classroom window, as well.)

Action: Invite children to paint on the plastic or window surface. Explain to them that this is a painting that two people create together. When one child paints a blue line, for example, the child on the other side will paint that same blue line on her side of the plastic/window, too. The children can take turns making their marks and responding with their marks and brushstrokes. Encourage children to try different strategies, such as using big strokes, dots, circles, swirls, and so on. You can add texture to the tempera paint by adding salt or sand to the paint. The children will notice how what feels bumpy or gritty on one side of the plastic/glass feels smooth on the other side. This noticing may lead to discussions about how we can notice what other people are feeling, even though we may not feel that same way ourselves.

Figure 8.3 Perspective Painting 1

Figure 8.4 Perspective Painting 2

Questions of Conscience

Goal: To explore with children their beliefs about what is acceptable, appropriate behavior in hypothetical situations

Materials: None needed, although young children may understand the concepts well using a book, such as *The Honest-to-Goodness Truth* (McKissack, 2000), or the fable about the boy who cried wolf, to anchor and launch their discussion

Action: Invite children to come to the rug or small table. (Note: this activity works well with small groups of children, to maximize opportunities for children to participate, though it can also be done with a large group.) You may wish to read a book or share the fable with the group first, noting that you are going to talk about what we do in certain situations.

The following questions are prompts that will elicit varying responses from the children:

◆ Is it ok to steal food if you can't afford to buy it?
◆ Is it ok to drive over the speed limit if you are rushing to the hospital?

- ◆ If you find a lost toy on the playground, how hard should you look for the owner? Is it ok to keep the toy if you can't find the owner?
- ◆ If a store cashier charges you less for something than the actual price, is it ok to keep quiet about it?

Explain to the children that sometimes different situations require different actions. We often judge people or actions before we know the whole story. How does our thinking change when we consider different reasons for people's actions? By engaging in these conversations, children will deepen their understanding of human behavior, learning that sometimes suspending our judgment opens possibilities for empathy and action, as appropriate.

Music, Movement, and Me

Goal: To expose children to different music and dance traditions that reflect the cultural backgrounds of children, families, and teachers at the school

Materials needed: Music from children and families—CDs, audio recordings, or live music are all wonderful options

Action: Send home a letter or email to families informing them that the class will be enjoying music and dance representing the many cultural backgrounds of classroom/school community members. Invite families to share music with the class through whatever channels are most convenient (e.g., bringing CDs into the classroom, playing an instrument for the class, sending a link or mp3 file via email). The local library is another excellent resource for locating and borrowing music, as well as books that will enhance the classroom library. Over the course of a week, or longer, dedicate time for the large group to listen to music together. Ask the children questions about what they notice and how they would describe the music, such as, "How does the music sound? Is it loud? Soft? Fast? Slow? Does it have a steady beat, or does the beat change throughout the song? What colors does the music remind you of? How does the music make you want to move?" Provide the children with scarves or pieces of cloth to use to mimic the beat or flow of the music, and invite them to move their bodies as well. This activity can also be used as a choice or center time activity, where children can listen to music together in small groups, or individually, depending on the music equipment and classroom space.

Extension: Invite family members to come into the classroom and share stories with the group about when and how this music is typically played in the family or broader culture.

A Closer Look: Responsibility for Others

Uma strode into the kindergarten classroom, ready to begin week six of her senior student teaching practicum with new resolve. She was determined to engage the children in an activity that would address the language-learning needs of several students and at the same time meet the standards for her math and science lesson plan requirements. She'd been enjoying her senior practicum very much, eagerly noticing the challenges that each student faced and framing these challenges as opportunities for her to strengthen her own skill set during the brief time she'd have the benefit of Ms. S.'s—her cooperating practitioner's—guidance and wisdom.

As she began unpacking her canvas bag of supplies, children filed past her, and she caught snippets of conversation from different conversations in progress:

". . . and my mom said I could use the iPad *only if* my sister didn't need it for *homework* . . ."

". . . the purple ones are better for stretching. The other ones break really easy . . ."

"Don't go near Gabriel! He hits people!"

This last comment stung. Uma had noticed for weeks how the children tended to shy away from Gabriel, a sturdy child with brown curly hair, deep brown eyes that were slightly magnified by his eyeglasses (which only made them sparkle more brightly, in Uma's opinion), and a dimple in his right cheek that appeared when he was deep in thought, clenching the inside of his cheek, or smiling. It pained Uma to see the children's reactions to Gabriel, as she truly believed that he was trying to connect with children in his own way. Gabriel's parents had told Ms. S. that Gabriel had attention deficit hyperactivity disorder (ADHD), but Ms. S. confided with Uma that she suspected that diagnosis to be incorrect. Ms. S. believed Gabriel to be somewhere on the autism spectrum, likely a highly functioning child with autism, perhaps Asperger's syndrome.

Uma had no sooner thought about this then she heard the voice of Principal Woodward wafting down the hallway:

"Gabriel! Buddy, you're going to need to wear this today. I can't let you sit in my office this morning, so I need you to put on your listening ears and wear this special vest. I wish I had a vest like this! Can you do this for me, buddy? I need to see that you're listening, Gabriel."

Gabriel walked into the room with his arms crossed over his chest, holding his Koopa figure—a favorite character among the children who knew about the Mario video game characters. Gabriel never went anywhere without his Koopa figure. Gabriel's brow was furrowed and he marched angrily over to the cubbies and sat in his cubby spot. Principal Woodward and Ms. S. came in the room together, and Ms. S. knelt down in front of Gabriel while Principal Woodward stood behind her, one hand on his hip, holding the vest, and one hand twisting the tiepin he had fastened to his necktie.

Uma listened to Ms. S. and Principal Woodward explain to Gabriel that he had one chance today to stay in the classroom, and if he couldn't "make it work" and focus during class, then he'd have to go home. Uma knew that Gabriel's parents were very concerned about Gabriel's socialization at school, as well as his academic progress. Because he often got in trouble for hitting or other behaviors, he often got pulled out of the classroom and therefore missed classroom academic work for several minutes of every day. While Gabriel's parents used the term ADHD as a loose explanation for Gabriel's behaviors, Uma believed that it was perhaps too scary for them to acknowledge Gabriel might instead have a different diagnosis—one that would carry a different stigma and require resources that they weren't aware of—thus, the unknown. The weighted vest had been suggested by the occupational therapist who had observed Gabriel as part of his Individualized Education Program (IEP) process. Everyone was hoping the vest would help Gabriel calm down and focus during work time in class.

***

After morning meeting, Ms. S. called the names of the children and they chose their center activities one by one. Uma noticed that Gabriel hadn't put on his weighted vest yet—it was flopped over the book rack behind where he was sitting at the art table. Uma picked up the vest as she joined him at the art table. She took a piece of paper and began drawing a picture of Koopa. Annaliese, a student in the class, saw Uma's drawing and exclaimed, "Oooh! Koopa!—look, Gabriel!" Gabriel looked at Uma's drawing and began watching her intently. Uma noticed that the dimple had appeared in his cheek again—a positive sign, in her opinion.

When she finished her drawing, Uma cut out the picture of Koopa and taped it to the vest. Annaliese asked, "Can I make one, too?" Uma passed some paper and markers to Annaliese and stood up to make room for Abdul, who had come over to see what was happening.

"Cool! I want to make one, too, Miss Uma!"

In the span of a few minutes, three children were busily working on Koopa drawings, and as they finished each one, Uma attached them to Gabriel's vest.

"Put it on, Gabriel!" squealed Annaliese. And to Uma's amazement, Gabriel did put on the vest.

"Gabriel, you look so cool!" Abdul said, looking Gabriel up and down. More children came over to admire Gabriel's vest, and Gabriel's smile made all of the teachers look at each other in wonder, and smile as well.

***

Gabriel wore the vest for the entire day, and his fellow classmates were noticeably more encouraging toward him, which, in turn, elicited different behavior from Gabriel. Or maybe it was the other way around—Uma couldn't be sure. All she knew was that it had been the best day Gabriel had had in a long time. She and Ms. S. took pictures to show Gabriel's parents and Principal Woodward, and they planned to incorporate this documentation into their upcoming IEP meetings. Uma hoped today was the first of many successful days to come.

When it came time for the children to clean up and get ready to leave, Ms. S. said to Gabriel, "Gabriel, I need you to take off your vest and hang it in your cubby."

Gabriel's face changed instantly, and he crossed his arms in front of his chest. "NO!" he said. He frowned and sat down in his cubby. Ms. S. knelt in front of him again and said calmly, "You can have it again tomorrow, Gabriel. It's not going any-where. The vest will be here again in the morning. It needs a rest now, too."

As soon as she heard the word "rest," Uma had an idea. "Why don't we make a bed for your vest, Gabriel?" She walked over to the dramatic play area and arranged some blocks in a rectangle. Annaliese and Abdul trotted over to her and Abdul said excitedly, "It's a volcano! Gabriel, your vest can rest in the volcano!" Abdul added some blocks and Annaliese grabbed a scarf from the clothes bin to make the "soft lava" for the volcano bed. Gabriel watched the activity unfolding before him, and when the bed was finished, he took Koopa out of the left chest pocket of the vest, then took the vest off and laid it delicately in the volcano bed.

As the children lined up to head to the bus and pick up area, Ms. S. touched Uma's shoulder and said, "I never thought he would wear that vest. This is one of those moments, Uma! Something important changed today. It may be different tomorrow, but I'm going to hold on to today for a long time. Thank you for that."

Resources

Children's Defense Fund
www.childrensdefense.org/

This organization has as its mission a healthy and successful life for children, supported by families and communities. Directed ably and lovingly by Marian Wright Edelman, CDF presents detailed reports and research and calls upon all of us to be actively engaged in ensuring that child development, justice, and welfare are priorities.

Making Caring Common
https://mcc.gse.harvard.edu/

A project anchored in the Harvard Graduate School of Education, MCC is a site for educators, families, and everyone committed to raising children who are "caring, responsible to their communities, and committed to justice." Articles, opportunities for social action, and many other resources engage visitors to the site with current as well as perennial topics to explore.

World Cultural Dance
www.fitforafeast.com/dance_cultural.htm

This website lets visitors discover folk songs and dances from around the world. Other areas on the site include songs and instruments, instructional videos, and cooking activities.

References

Desautels, L. (2016). Brains in pain cannot learn! *Edutopia*. Retrieved from www.edutopia.org/blog/brains-in-pain-cannot-learn-lori-desautels?utm_source=twitter&utm_medium=socialflow

Hutchby, I., & Moran-Ellis, J. (2001). *Children, technology, and culture: The impacts of technologies in children's everyday lives*. New York, NY: Routledge.

Langworthy, S.E. (2015). *Bridging the relationship gap: Connecting with children facing adversity*. St. Paul, MN: Redleaf Press.

Lionni, L. (1963). *Swimmy*. New York, NY: Alfred A. Knopf.

McKissack, P.C. (2003). *The honest-to-goodness truth*. New York: Aladdin Paperbacks.

National Association for the Education of Young Children (NAEYC). (2011). *Code of ethical conduct and statement of commitment*. [Position Statement]. Retrieved from www.naeyc.org/sites/default/files/globally-shared/downloads/PDFs/resources/position-statements/Ethics%20Position%20Statement2011_09202013update.pdf)

National Scientific Council on the Developing Child. (2004). *Young children develop in an environment of relationships*. Cambridge, MA: Center on the Developing Child. Retrieved from https://developingchild.harvard.edu/resources/wp1/

Newberg, A., & Waldman, M.R. (2006). *Why we believe what we believe: Uncovering our biological need for meaning, spirituality, and truth*. New York, NY: Free Press.

O'Keeffe, G.S., & Clarke-Pearson, K. (2011). The impact of social media on children, adolescents, and families. *Pediatrics, 127*(4). Retrieved from http://pediatrics.aappublications.org/content/127/4/800

Prensky, M. (2001). Digital natives, digital immigrants. *On the Horizon, 9*(5), 1–6. MCB University Press.

Rodriguez, V., & Fitzpatrick, M. (2014). *The teaching brain: An evolutionary trait at the heart of education*. New York, NY: The New Press.

Subrahmanyam, K., Kraut, R.E., Greenfield, P.M., & Gross, E.F. (2000). The impact of home computer use on children's activities and development. *The Future of Children, 10*(2), 123–144.

Turkle, S. (2015). *Reclaiming conversation: The power of talk in a digital age*. New York, NY: Penguin Press.

Willard, C. (2017). *Raising resilience: The wisdom and science of happy families and thriving children*. Boulder, CO: Sounds True.

9

Advocacy and Action

The early childhood years are a special period in human development, when joy and wonder in everyday discoveries contribute to patterns and relationships that influence people over the course of their lifetimes. This can sound both exciting and daunting to early childhood teachers, because teachers who work and learn with young children and their families assume a large responsibility and demonstrate vital commitment to the children in the classroom, and to our larger society. Throughout this book, information has been provided to enrich teachers' understandings of the protective factors—*grit*, *resilience*, and *motivation*—that help strengthen children along their respective pathways to healthy, successful adulthood. For example, a consistent theme in research literature spanning many decades came from children themselves—they reported having a feeling or faith that their lives made sense, that certain odds could be overcome, and that their lives had purpose. "The men and women who made successful transitions into adulthood and midlife had a more internal locus of control at age 18 than their peers who developed coping problems at age 40. They expressed a strong belief that they could control their fate by their own actions" (Werner & Smith, 2001, p. 151).

Redefining Theory and Practice

Teachers often believe that they have to control or "manage" the class-room environment. A first step toward redefining the relationships between theory and practice is to acknowledge that there is actually very little about human development that we, as teachers, can control. We can, however, position ourselves in the classroom as co-learners, as advocates, and as active and engaged listeners who work in a system of relationships to empower children. The words of educator and author Loris Malaguzzi reflect this stance:

> The history a child has inside them is not just a story of the present; it is the story of the past, and it is the story of the future. Where ideological pressure exists in children's education and intimidates children with its authority, with its exclusivity and the one way, then clearly education is not being done, certainly liberal education is not being done. This is education that is not inclusive, and where we are not freeing children, not respecting the rhythms nature could and would allow if they could move very freely without brakes and without stops.
>
> (Loris Malaguzzi, as cited in Cagliari, Castagnetti, Guidici, Rinaldi, Vecchi, & Moss, 2016, p. 266)

If teachers consider their work through the lens of systems and relationships, teaching young children becomes a collaborative act. And research in developmental theory supports the idea that humans are literally wired to seek out human connections.

Attachment

One example from the field of neuroscience that underscores this notion is the existence of "mirror neurons," which are, simply put, brain cells that respond similarly when we perform an action and when we witness someone else doing an action.

There are social implications for these microscopic biological cells, because the biological mechanisms can influence social responses:

> Our brains practice doing actions we merely observe in others, as if we're doing them ourselves. If you've ever watched an intense fan at a game, you know what we are talking about— he twitches at every mistake, aching to give his own motor actions to the players on the field. When we see players run,

jump, or kick, it is not only our visual cortex or even the part of our brain that thinks about what we are observing that is activated, but also the parts of our brain that would be activated if we ourselves were running, jumping, or kicking.

(Christakis & Fowler, 2009, p. 39)

Some neuroscientists argue that individual human beings are always searching for direct connections with other humans, and that we "are neutrally programmed to complete ourselves *only* in genuine relationships with other human beings" (Slade, 2012, p. 23). They contend that this "programming is so powerful and so deeply embedded in the primate fabric of our brains" (Slade, 2012, p. 23) that we seek out substitutes (e.g., smartphones, social media sites) when we can't establish or sustain satisfying connections with other people.

There are echoes here of Harry Harlow's controversial experiments with rhesus monkeys (1950s), in which newborn monkeys were provided with substitute "mother" monkeys constructed of wire and other objects—one cloth-covered, softer model, and one wood and wire model (see www.simplypsychology.org/attachment.html#harlow). The newborn monkeys showed a clear preference for the softer maternal figure, and they experienced physical and social-emotional effects depending on which monkey they were placed with in their respective crates.

There are also traces of Albert Bandura's social learning theory to consider. Bandura argues that observing some action or activity is enough to influence children's thinking and behavior. In his classic Bobo doll experiments (see https://simplypsychology.org/bobo-doll.html), Bandura illustrated how children could observe adults' behavior and that behavior would therefore influence their own play.

For teachers of young children, sometimes the most important action can be to simply slow down and demonstrate compassion or close listening.

Although it may seem heavy-handed when most of the class does understand how to share and think of others, we must remember that these social and emotional skills are skills to be learned. Just like teaching fractions or how to make predictions, we must scaffold our students' learning with direct instruction, differentiation, and an abundance of laughter and patience.

(Buckley, 2015, p. 69)

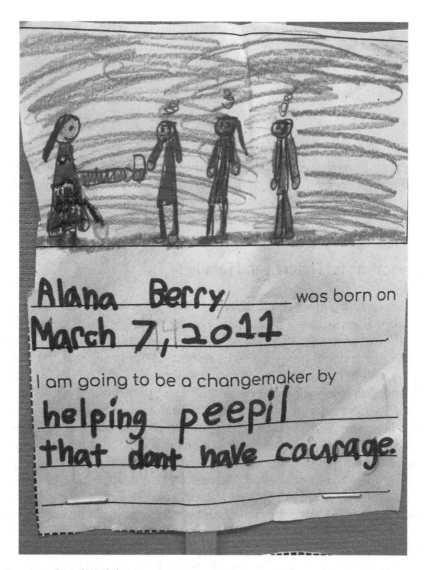

Figure 9.1 Peepil Worksheet

The human desire for connection is strong, and the act of developing trust can take time. It can be "an awkward, time-consuming process, like forming friendships" (Slade, 2012, p. 30).

Although most teachers are already aware of the direct effects they have on children, families, and colleagues, they don't often consider that

> everything we think, feel, do, or say can spread far beyond the people we know. . . . In a kind of social chain reaction, we can

be deeply affected by events we do not witness that happen to people we do not know. It is as if we can feel the pulse of the social world around us and respond to its persistent rhythms. As part of a social network, we transcend ourselves, for good or ill, and become a part of something much larger. We are connected.

(Christakis & Fowler, 2009, p. 30)

In the sections that follow, including the activities and resources at the end of this chapter, information is provided to help guide your own discovery and flexing of the muscle that encourages advocacy and action.

Advocating for Children and Families

Educator and author Linda Darling-Hammond notes that much of what predicts students' abilities to engage with academic work is the "ability to focus your attention, to manage your emotions, to be resilient when you run into problems, to be resourceful and engage with others to get and give information" (Aspen Institute, 2017, p. 15). She proposes that while these social-emotional skills tend to result in stronger academic performance, they are also the behaviors people need outside of the classroom. She adds that "[i]t's no different for teachers . . . [who] need to be aware of their emotions, manage and adjust their stress levels, collaborate with others, and create good interpersonal relationships with students, colleagues, and parents" (Aspen Institute, 2017, p. 15).

So if teachers are humans who are therefore wired to be connected, then the networks that they create and participate within do not belong to any one individual—the work and energy is shared by everyone in the network. In this way, teachers can participate in social networks that will benefit children, families, and the field of education. Finding or creating an avenue to effect change is similar to caring for a community garden, in that there is potential for many individuals and groups to enjoy it, and that also means people must work together to ensure it remains healthy. "This means that social networks require tending, by individuals, by groups, and by institutions" (Christakis & Fowler, 2009, p. 31).

Tending to early childhood educators' social and emotional learning is therefore a critical aspect of advocating for children. Just as teacher preparation curricula and professional development programs address how children learn and develop, these same offerings must provide opportunities for educators to practice this work themselves, and observe and discuss with their peers. At all levels of school buildings, literally and figuratively, teachers, staff, and administrators must be given opportunities to develop their own social-emotional competence so that they can model and scaffold these same skills for students in classrooms (Aspen Institute, 2017).

Family Engagement

The network of advocates for children also extends to parents and families, and this includes what happens outside of the walls of any classroom or school building. It is essential to expand the traditional notion of family involvement to consider home activities as well as school activities. In an effort to truly empower families to be children's most effective advocates, educators need to understand the impact of family and culture on children's development:

> We are not concerned with activities traditionally equated with school success, that is, many books and toys in the home, frequent attendance at cultural activities, and so on. What we mean by home activities are intangibles: *consistent communication, high expectations, pride, understanding,* and *enthusiasm* for their children's school experiences. The view that poor parents and those who speak another language or come from a dominated culture are unable to provide environments that promote learning can lead to condescending practices that reject the skills and resources they already have.
>
> (Nieto, 2000, p. 333)

Families are more confident advocating for issues that matter to them when they perceive themselves as strong and valued members of the community. Contributing to group activism activities about specific issues that matter to their children is empowering to all family members, and this teaches everyone involved that people can make life better by working together.

A terrific example of motivation to inspire advocacy may be seen in the work of the Children's Defense Fund. This organization works to ensure equity for all children in terms of financial, social, educational, spiritual, and health-related domains. In its recent report, *The State of America's Children® 2017*, readers are provided with the following call to action:

> Whether you describe yourself as a teacher, child advocate, policymaker, policy wonk, college professor, faith leader, parent

or grandparent, a millennial eager to make life better for your younger siblings, or a member of the media, we ask you to use [these data], combined where possible with stories of real children, to inform your conversations and effectively make the case for policies, programs, and strategies for improving the odds for children in your states and nationwide. We must keep moving forward.

(Children's Defense Fund, 2017, p. i)

Since its origins over 40 years ago, the CDF has persisted in efforts to elevate children's living conditions and join forces with local, state, and federal agencies to extend the reach of the work.

Pushing Back to Move Forward

Changing systems that have been in existence for hundreds of years and have roots firmly entrenched in the political, social, and economic topography of the United States is no easy feat. Actualizing the concepts of *grit*, *resilience*, and *motivation* in educational settings is one act of advocacy that teachers and children may engage in every day. As teachers teach and empower young children in classrooms, they are constructing with children the necessary tools to spur resilient spirits into action—to embody grit. Author Taylor Clark (2011) invites people to meet challenges with a similar attitude:

> [I]f you want to give your amygdala a chance to get over a fear, you must expose yourself to the things and ideas that scare you. . . . Just get in the habit of moving *toward* your fears rather than running away. When you do so, even "failures" become successes, each exposure two steps forward to one step back.
>
> (p. 276)

Children benefit when critical conversations about education shift "from a win/lose, deficit approach to one that is win/win and asset-based. It sees difference as a resource, not a problem" (DeRosa & Johnson, 2002, p. 8).

Many educators and advocates believe that schools—and education in general—hold the most promise for a healthy democracy to thrive. Imperative to the success of this democracy, however, is equal, equitable access to all members of the population, including those for whom access is routinely denied due to race, disability, socioeconomic status, or other factors (Nathan, 2017). "Now more than ever, it is imperative that schools be places where students feel welcome and safe. Of equal importance, students need to feel valued, respected, and known by the adults at the school" (Krovetz, 2008, p. x).

If teachers aspire to influence how society works, they can begin by building connections between individuals. Doing so helps children "understand how interconnections and interactions between people give rise to wholly new aspects of human experience that are not present in the individuals themselves . . . or the world we inhabit" (Christakis & Fowler, 2009, p. 32). In a delightful and moving animated film, *My Life as a Zucchini* (described in detail in the Resources section below), the children speak with an adult about her unconditional love for her newborn child, asking her if she'll love the child:

> Even . . .
> Even if he's ugly?
> Even if he smells bad?
> Even if he cries all the time?
> Even if he wets the bed?
> Even if he's bad at school?
> Even if he's dumb?
> Even if he eats like a pig?
> Even if he forgets his name and his feet are stinky?
> Even if he's super annoying and won't stop screaming?
> Even if he farts?
> Even if he scribbles on the walls?
> Even if he wants to be a cop?
> Even if . . .
> Even if his neck is long, like a giraffe?
> Even if he is a punk?
>
> (Karli & Barras, 2016)

Teachers convey this same kind of awareness and validation to the children with whom they work. Compassionate, empowering teaching goes beyond simply caring for children—it extends to seeing them, listening to them, and knowing them and their families more deeply. It is hard to be a teacher. And it is for you, and those you are connected with in the interest of children's learning and development, that the words *grit*, *resilience*, and *motivation* inspire action and advocacy.

You've got this.

Turning Ideas Into Action

Seeds of Compassion, Roots of Connection

Goal: To recognize emotions and situations that evoke/involve these emotions

Materials needed: Photographs of children's faces displaying different emotions (e.g., happy, sad, mad, excited, disgusted, surprised, afraid). Photographs may be of the children in the class or ones found in magazines, books, or online sources. (Note: an online search, typing "children's emotions" into the browser bar and then clicking "images," provides access to many resources that may be utilized for this activity.) Mirrors—handheld mirrors are most useful, but a large mirror is also fine and can be used by several children at once, which adds a different element to this activity.

Action: It is interesting to notice that a label that is put on one photo may not reflect all students' understandings of that emotion. Invite children to look at a photo of a child displaying an emotion. Ask the children to guess what this child is feeling and to share what feeling they think the photo displays. You may hear many similar answers, and you may also hear different answers shared. You may wish to ask clarifying questions, such as "What is it about ____'s facial expression that makes you think she is ____?" Next, ask the children to make faces that reflect the specific emotion displayed in the photo. Some of the children may make a very similar face, and some children may look very different from what the image displays. They may verbalize that they don't look the same as the picture because they don't actually feel that specific emotion in that moment. This is an excellent opportunity to point out that we can recognize someone else's emotions, and that we don't need to also *feel* the same way as that person. That is, in fact, showing compassion for someone else. The subsequent conversations about how or why an image conveys specific emotions—and what that means to us as we notice these emotions—are most informative!

Extension: Children can use art/recyclable materials to create faces with glue and paint. These creations may be combined into a book that captures the various faces that correspond to different emotions. On a smaller scale, children can create "matching" cards in which children match the emotion displayed on a card with the word that describes it. (This can further contribute to interesting and rich discussions and understandings about how we perceive and respond to people.)

Ready, Set, Active!

Goal: To introduce children to the concepts of activism, social justice, and democracy

Materials: Camera; sketchbooks or paper that children may use to draw upon; pencils

Action: Young children are often interested in how their parents vote in a voting booth or get involved in activities such as marches or rallies.

Figure 9.2 At the Women's March

While they may not understand the complexities of local, state, or national government, they readily understand how they feel when something is fair or unjust. You may discuss with the class the concept of voting and how that works in your community. For example, some communities have participatory budgeting processes, in which residents (including children!) have a say in how a specified portion of the budget is allocated. (See http://pb.cambridgema.gov for one example of the process and outcomes.)

Ask students to think about ideas they have for changes they would like to see in their classroom, school, or neighborhood. Depending on the scope of the ideas—new colors of paint for art activities, more accessible parking spaces for families with physical disabilities, changes to immigration legislation—invite a local resident or elected official to speak with the students, or take a class walk to a local government office. The local library is often a wonderful resource for picture books on the topic of government, free passes to museums, and other activities related to civic engagement.

On a field trip or class walk, the children can record their observations by drawing during a break for snack or resting. In addition to drawings, children's ideas and inspirations can be recorded by teachers and/or family members in the form of letters to be sent to elected officials. See if you receive a response from an elected official! It is a powerful experience for children to see and hear that their ideas were heard and respected by someone in a position of decision-making authority, and this reflects in a concrete format how exercising one's right to vote can have a positive impact on a community.

Respect, Even If . . . Time Capsule

Goal: To understand ways that classroom community members share beliefs, share values, and convey respect for each other and the environment

Materials: Waterproof and/or airtight box (one per classroom or group, if this activity is used with smaller groups of children); markers; magazines; glue sticks or glue; index cards or small pieces of paper; pencils/pens; newspaper; other items as determined by the group

Action: Discuss with the class the idea of a time capsule. Invite children to share ideas about why people would create a time capsule, and what they would want to put into a class time capsule that would convey to others the respect that these children have for each other and for their classroom.

Ask children to think about who might look at or find their time capsule. What are some of the big ideas that they have learned and discussed in class that they wish to share with others? Invite children to decorate the container/box with paper, markers, and/or images that they take from magazines and glue onto the container. Over the course of the project, while children are decorating the container, invite them to next draw pictures and write (or dictate) letters on the index cards for future readers/finders of the capsule contents. The cards may be used to respond to a prompt, such as, "I respect my ___ even if . . ." and/or children may develop their own ideas.

When the container is decorated and drawings and writings are complete, the group can determine whether there is anything else they wish to add to the capsule. They might want to include newspaper stories or clippings that depict relevant current events, artwork, photographs, or other items of their choosing. Once the container is determined to be complete, have the children seal the box. Mark the completion of the activity with a celebratory photograph to commemorate the event. Depending upon the timeline for opening the box, the children may be present for the opening. If children are no longer at the school when the container is opened, sending photos and/or messages that communicate the experience of those who opened the capsule is a terrific way to share the experience!

A Closer Look: Advocacy and Action

Mrs. Garver and Ms. Piteri co-teach a kindergarten class of 22 4- to 5-year-olds in Boston, MA. In the fall, when they prepared to launch their curriculum unit on the U.S. Constitution, they designated one wall of their classroom as the documentation wall, where they would use documentation both as a reflection tool to revisit learning with the children and also as a timeline to display the next steps in their group's learning process. The documentation wall was a new addition to the already familiar places in the classroom, such as the Peace Corner, the Math/Science area, the Word Wall, and Dramatic Play space. The teachers spent several planning sessions discussing how they would display snippets of dialogue, photos of children, narrative descriptions, and samples of students' work from left to right, as someone would read a book.

The two teachers decided that the "hook" they would use to engage the children in their topic was Rules. Since the beginning of any school year included numerous discussions and role-playing that resulted in co-constructed rules and class norms, this seemed a natural way to engage the students. For the first few days, the children explored children's books and engaged in conversations, and the teachers took photos of the children reading and playing together. Children drew pictures of their own interpretations of rules in their families, schools, and community environments, and the class discussed many facets of rules. Some topics raised in class discussions were: *What is a rule? Who makes the rules?* and *When is it ok to break the rules?* The teachers used photographs, samples of children's work, and quotes from discussions to remind children of their previous ideas and to extend the work in new directions.

To build on the children's understanding of rules and the U.S. Constitution, the teachers decided to introduce the children to several community members whose daily work involved keeping people safe and questioning and/or validating the rules. For example, Officer Muñoz, a female resource officer who worked in the local middle school, and Mr. Jefferson, an attorney who specialized in immigration law, visited the class. Each person shared with the children some of their daily work tasks, challenges, and triumphs. During the discussions it was decided that over the next several months the children would interview more community members, and they divided the topic of rules into safety rules, respect rules, and caring rules.

***

In mid-January, a scheduled class visitor, who was the parent of a child who'd been in the class during the previous year, entered the room looking rather upset. "I'm not sure that I can get through this without losing it," the parent told Mrs. Garver. He explained that on his way to the school, he heard a story on the radio about alleged "vulgar" comments that President Trump made during the course of a meeting with senators. The parent, Mr. Vilasson, told her that he had immigrated to the United States from Haiti with his family when he was just 5 years old, "the same age as these children!" He choked over his words as he accepted Mrs. Garver's hand, saying, "We work hard, we contribute to the community, and this is how the leader of our country refers to us. How can we expect anything to be any different than it is if this is the example a 'leader' [using air quotes] sets?" Some of the children had wandered over to Mrs. Garver and Mr. Vilasson, and their faces showed concern and curiosity. Ms. Piteri and Mrs. Garver exchanged a look and Ms. Piteri played the listening chimes to invite the group's attention. "We're going to shift gears, friends," she said. "Let's come over to the rug to speak with our guest, Mr. Vilasson." The students came over to the rug, and Mrs. Garver took a deep breath, starting a conversation that she hadn't planned, but knowing she could trust the process.

After introducing Mr. Vilasson to the group, noting that he works for the company that is in charge of supplying gas to all of the buildings and homes in the city, Mrs. Garver invited Mr. Vilasson to share how he was feeling with the class. "I'm frankly feeling rather sad right now," he said. "I wish I had a different answer!" He smiled.

"What made you sad?" asked Johnna, her eyebrows knitted into a crease on her forehead.

Mrs. Garver answered, "Remember when we first learned about rules, waaaay back in September? Do you remember how we decided that some rules keep us safe, some rules show respect for others and the environment, and some rules show caring for others? Well, Mr. Vilasson heard something on the radio about the president of the United States and some things that he said. It makes me wonder whether he was thinking about the rules for people's feelings."

Ms. Piteri joined the conversation, as some children began talking excitedly at the same time. "He basically called some countries poop," she said. This comment stopped all conversation, and the children looked at Ms. Piteri—some wide-eyed, some with mouths open, some with eyebrows raised incredulously. Even Mr. Vilasson looked surprised, and then he nodded his head and looked around at the students.

"My family and I came to the United States when I was the same age as you are," he said. "My father borrowed money from his uncle to pay for us to come on a boat, and he worked days and many nights for years to pay his uncle back, because my parents believed that this country could offer us more opportunity, more food, more safety, than our country could at that time." Children began asking questions and sharing about the various countries that their families were from, and Mrs. Garver took one of the classroom's persona dolls—Esther (who is known to the class as a Black girl who speaks Haitian Creole)—from the top of the bookshelf. She told the students, "Esther has feelings and ideas just like all of us. How do you think she feels to hear Mr. Vilasson's story?"

"Sad, and maybe scared," said one student.

"It sounds like me and Farah," said another student.

"What sounds like you and Farah?" Mrs. Garver asked Rosaline.

"My mom and Farah's mom were talking about this yesterday, too. They were both mad."

"So Esther might feel mad, like your mom and Farah's mom," said Mrs. Garver. "What can we do? It is ok for the president to hurt people's feelings?"

"Our country has free speech, so people can say what they want," said Peter.

"But not to hurt people! It's not ok to hurt people!" stated Emile. "Isn't that right, Mrs. Garver?"

"Hmmm . . . as I listen to you, I'm noticing that you sound angry. How come you are so angry?" Several students shared their answers, and Mrs. Garver responded, "You know, it's true that we do have free speech in our country, *and* it's true that it's not ok to hurt people. Remember when we talked about the U.S. Constitution? We talked about rules, and who gets to make rules, and when it's ok to break the rules. We live in a country where we can see something that we don't like and we can say and *do* something about it."

"So what are we going to do?" asked Mr. Vilasson.

***

Throughout the rest of that day and in the days that followed, the children and adults generated ideas about how they might address what they perceived as disrespectful, derogatory statements made by the president. These ideas were shared in conversations, drawings, and writing. Mrs. Garver and Ms. Piteri posted documentation on their documentation wall so that children and families could follow the thoughts and progress. Since they had decided to shift the focus from their planned curriculum to the children's emerging ideas about addressing discrimination, the teachers sent an email to families describing the actions that the children had proposed, including sending letters to the president.

Mrs. Garver purchased blank postcards from the neighborhood post office, and the children drew pictures and wrote messages on the postcards during their classroom choice time. Mrs. Garver encouraged the students to illustrate the postcards with images that reflected their feelings or identified specific values that they shared in the classroom. For instance, one child drew a rainbow and dictated the words "We are all happy together" to Ms. Piteri, because she wanted her postcard "to be able to make sad people happy." Other children decided to draw heroes that they admired, noting the different powers that they had and how the different powers made them stronger together. The process of writing and drawing on the postcards led to discussions about a field trip to the post office. Children who had finished their postcards created signs that they would carry as they walked to and back from the post office. Noting the connections to content areas, the teachers communicated with families and administrators (using blog posts and a class website) about how their postcard project was leading to greater phonemic awareness, as evident in children's learning about letter sounds and initials, and applied math and social studies skills, as evident in their drawings and understandings of the process of sending mail.

***

Everyone in the class was very invested in their individual and group work on the postcards, and every day Mrs. Garver suggested that they look at their class's documentation up to that point to review their group's journey from the beginning of the "rules" conversations to the current time. Simple prompts sparked lively conversations as children remembered their individual and group learning processes. As the end of the week and their field trip grew closer, Mrs. Garver and Ms. Piteri grew more excited.

On the day of the field trip, a reporter from the local newspaper came and took pictures of the children lining up with family members. Children held signs that expressed sentiments such as "ALL PEOPLE ARE IMPORTANT!" "FANMI MWEN SE ESPESYAL AK FÒ!" ("My family is special and strong!") and "RESPETARME, RESPETAR MI PERRO!" ("Respect me, respect my dog!") The class—including teachers, some family members, and some community members—marched together to the post office three blocks away from the school. The postal worker, Ms. Ngo, was expecting the children and greeted them warmly: "Good morning, amazing activists!" Ms. Garver took pictures of each child placing their postcard in the mail slot and sent the photos to their families at the end of the day, along with a blog post that described the events leading up to the march, as well as the march itself.

***

These experiences contributed to a common knowledge base constructed by the children, teachers, families, and community members. Mrs. Garver and Ms. Piteri decided to help the group transition to a unit focusing on "real-life" heroes. "Can you think of people in your community who are community helpers?" asked Mrs. Garver. She explained that the children had used their powers of thinking, feeling, and acting to help their community. She noted that there are people in their community who also use their skills every day to help the city run smoothly and safely. The children identified firefighters, doctors, and teachers as examples of real-life heroes who use their safety, respect, and caring skills to help people, and Mrs. Garver invited a female firefighter to the class as their first guest expert for the unit.

Resources

Defending the Early Years
www.deyproject.org

This organization promotes healthy child development through advocacy efforts aimed at "the rights and needs of young children." Experts in the field of early childhood education provide insights and strategies to address school reform, assessments, and the importance and power of play. Toolkits and publications are available for viewing and dissemination.

My Life as a Zucchini
http://mylifeasazucchini.com

This is an amazing animated film about a boy whose mother dies suddenly, leaving him an orphan. After his mother's sudden death at the beginning of the film, Zucchini meets a kind police officer who brings him to a new home—a foster home inhabited by other orphans his age. This French film (soon to be released in an English version) demonstrates grit, resilience, and motivation and is a delight for children and those who love them.

Save the Children

www.savethechildren.org

Believing that all children deserve "a future," this organization works in the U.S. and around the world to provide children basic health and educational needs, as well as hope. Programs include onetime services and trainings that empower children, families, and communities. In 2016, this organization was able to provide support to over 157 million children, and one-third of those were reached directly by volunteers and staff working in these valuable programs.

References

Aspen Institute. (2017). *How learning happens: Supporting students' social, emotional, and academic development.*

Buckley, M.A. (2015). *Sharing the blue crayon: How to integrate social, emotional, and literacy learning.* Portland, ME: Stenhouse Publishers.

Cagliari, P., Castagnetti, M., Guidici, C., Rinaldi, C., Vecchi, V., & Moss, P. (2016). *Loris Malaguzzi and the schools of Reggio Emilia: A selection of his writings and speeches, 1945–1993.* New York, NY: Routledge.

Children's Defense Fund. (2017). *The state of America's children® 2017 report.* Retrieved from http://www.childrensdefense.org/library/state-of-americas-children/

Christakis, N.A., & Fowler, J.H. (2009). *Connected: How your friends' friends' friends affect everything you feel, think, and do.* New York, NY: Back Bay Books.

Clark, T. (2011). *Nerve: Poise under pressure, serenity under stress, and the brave new science of fear and cool.* New York, NY: Little, Brown and Company.

DeRosa, P., & Johnson, U. (2002). The 10Cs: A model of diversity awareness and social change. *The brown papers: Essays of reflection and analysis.* 6(5). Boston, MA: Women's Theological Center.

Karli, M. (Producer), & Barras, C. (Director). (2016). *My life as a zucchini (Ma vie de courgette)* [Motion Picture]. France: Rita Productions.

Krovetz, M.L. (2008). *Fostering resilience: Expecting all students to use their minds and hearts well, 2/e.* Thousand Oaks, CA: Corwin Press.

Nathan, L.F. (2017). *When grit isn't enough: A high school principal examines how poverty and inequality thwart the college-for-all promise.* Boston, MA: Beacon Press.

Nieto, S. (2000). *Affirming diversity: The sociopolitical context of multicultural education.* New York, NY: Longman.

Slade, G. (2012). *The big disconnect: The story of technology and loneliness.* New York, NY: Prometheus Books.

Werner, E.E., & Smith, R.S. (2001). *Journeys from childhood to midlife: Risk, resilience, and recovery.* Ithaca, NY: Cornell University Press.